MORAL LAW IN CHRISTIAN SOCIAL ETHICS

MORAL LAW
IN CHRISTIAN
SOCIAL ETHICS

WALTER G. MUELDER

JOHN KNOX PRESS
RICHMOND, VIRGINIA

Library of Congress Catalog Card Number: 66-15972
© M. E. Bratcher 1966
Printed in the United States of America
3574 (WB) 270

Contents

Preface

This book about moral law in the field of Christian social ethics deals with laws of autonomy, values, persons, community, and the metaphysical or divine context of moral choice. Such laws direct choosing and do not of themselves resolve personal predicaments or the pressing social dilemmas of our time. As the first chapter explains there are several types of moral law. The type expounded here presents the norms which ought to be coherently obeyed in making decisions. Often confusion reigns because less than the whole range of moral laws under consideration is applied to a complex moral situation. An incompletely thought out decision may turn out to be a wrong or irresponsible one. It may have tragic effects.

One illustration may suffice to introduce the central concern of the book, though it does not appeal to specifically Christian norms. William L. Lawrence, science editor emeritus of *The Times,* and the only journalist permitted to witness the test of the first atomic bomb at Alamogordo and the only newspaperman to fly with the atomic mission over Nagasaki, asked leading representatives of science and the military two questions on the twentieth anniversary of the first demonstration. The questions were: "Why did you help make the bomb?" and "Knowing what you do now, would you do the same again?"[1]

The men whose responses were reported included J. Robert Oppenheimer, Edward Teller, Eugene P. Wigner, Leslie R. Groves, Emilio Segrè, John J. McCloy, and Luis W. Alvarez. Needless to say there was no clear consensus among these persons who had had a part in the original project. None of the respondents was an absolute pacifist or a religious objector to war as such. Of special interest are the categories of moral law or ethical factors to which they appealed or made reference. This is evident from characteristic statements which are quoted without relation to the persons making them.

The judgments and evaluations include the following: "To develop the bomb was right. To drop it was wrong." "Probably a settlement could have been reached by peaceful means." "An emergency does not eliminate any individual's responsibility, choice or conscience." "I had no sense of guilt, since I did not make the decision." "It is true we didn't need to bomb to win, but we needed it to save American lives." "Under the circumstances at the time, yes." "The President had hardly any alternative." "I am absolutely convinced that had we said they could keep the Emperor, together with the threat of the atomic bomb, they would have accepted and we would never have had to drop the bomb. . . . Then our position before the world would have been better." "The world has not had a major war in the past 20 years, and . . . most responsible people feel the risk of a World War III has diminished steadily with time in these same years. I am confident that both these admirable situations are directly traceable to the existence of nuclear weapons." "I have a deep, continuing, haunting sense of the damage done to European culture by the two world wars. The existence of the bomb has reduced the chance of World War III and has given us valid hope."

The main question is whether a system of moral laws obediently adhered to would bring coherence into ethical reflection on problems like the above. Would Christian ethics be soundly guided into making discriminate judgments in situations like this? What kinds of moral laws would be required to be situationally adequate with respect to choices about atomic bombs, or experimentation on human beings, or the questions raised by automation, or the moral problems of population control?

When one analyzes the responses to the two questions raised by William L. Lawrence one finds that they include such appeals, norms, and ethical factors as the following: (1) available alternatives, (2) consequences both immediate and long-range, (3) scope or range of values to be considered, (4) controlling ideals, (5) the values of the concrete or specific situation, (6) ultimate and proximate goals, (7) individual responsibility, (8) an ideal of community, society, or culture, (9) the social role of the decision-maker, or the differentiation of roles, (10) a conception of the most inclusive end, and (11) devotion to the community. These do not exhaust the list of analyzable factors. It is instructive as well as interesting that no one person included all of these in his evaluation. Many questions for philosophical and Christian ethics and for an interdisciplinary Christian social ethics are suggested by these factors and their relationships to one another.

None of the scientists or military men cited above appealed to any uniquely religious or Christian factor in his ethical reflection. What is the relationship, if any, between Christian ethics and social ethics in terms of moral law? Are Christian ethics and moral philosophy mutually exclusive? Do all responsible Christian decisions about complex and serious moral problems presuppose some structure of moral law even when the relativity of each situation is recognized and acknowledged?

The present book is a companion volume to my previous publication *Foundations of the Responsible Society*. These two volumes embrace both theoretical questions and concrete areas of social responsibility. In recent years the popularity of contextual or situational ethics has challenged the validity and relevance of universal principles or moral laws. Some Christian ethicists have repudiated moral philosophy entirely. On the other hand, there has been a revival of interest in the natural moral law tradition. This invites a reconsideration or reformulation of moral law theory.

In presenting a study of moral law in relation to Christian social ethics, this book makes no claim to theological or philosophical completeness. There are many issues in Christian and philosophical ethics which are not posed. What is attempted is a vindication of moral laws of the type proposed more than thirty years ago by Edgar S. Brightman in his book *Moral Laws*. That book suffered from the economic stringencies of publication ventures in the Great Depression and failed to receive the attention it deserved. Today, in an era marked by the relativities and skepticism of contextualism and situational ethics, the time may be ripe for a new look at a system of moral law which has a concern for the relevant values of concrete situations as the subject of *one* of its laws, the law of specification. In this sense existentialism is commanded by moral law. But this law does not stand alone.

In *Foundations of the Responsible Society* the key term is a "middle axiom" which bears an important relationship to the moral laws expounded herein. The idea of the responsible society is defined as follows: "A responsible society is one where freedom is the freedom of men who acknowledge responsibility to justice and public order, and where those who hold political authority or economic power are responsible for its exercise to God and the people whose welfare is affected by it."[2]

This "middle axiom" is itself a coherent composite of other concepts, axioms, or principles like freedom, justice, equality, respect for personality, authority, power, community, welfare, and responsibility to God and the people. The natural law tradition has often presented as "natural" moral law what is really a culture-saturated middle axiom. A middle axiom mediates between ultimate ideal goods or principles, on the one hand, and concrete programs of ethical commands, on the other. Such axioms are more specific and concrete than ultimate ideals or norms and less specific or concrete than particular decisions in particular situations. "Middle axioms" may also serve to build bridges between empirical generalizations in the behavioral sciences and philosophical or theological ethics. A middle axiom is not arithmetically in the middle but it mediates between the poles indicated above. Indeed, there may be several levels of generalization or abstraction in this middle range of moral propositions. They serve to provide guidelines for action. In the construction of "middle axioms" in Christian social ethics, Christian ethics, philosophical moral laws, and empirical generalizations are employed.

The moral laws are normative laws of choice. They are the principles of responsible decision. Any formulation of supposed natural law with substantive moral content and any middle axiom or any guideline principle for action *ought* to be consistent and coherent with the proposed system of moral laws. Of themselves they prescribe no code of conduct, but they comprise the rational normative structure of all truly ethical choice. The analysis will point out that even the sharpest critics of moral philosophy appeal to some of these laws. Full moral responsibility depends on their systematic and coherent employment.

I

MORAL LAW
AND CHRISTIAN SOCIAL ETHICS

A. INTRODUCTION: TYPES OF MORAL LAW

The main purpose of this book is to develop an idea of moral law. Moral laws are of several types. There is prescriptive or positive moral law. Such law may be found in moral codes and these codes may be of several types. They may be classified in terms of their proximate or ultimate source. They may also be classified according to their authority or sanction. The idea of moral law developed in this book is not prescriptive. It is not a code of positive law.

Moral law may be conceived as "natural" moral law. Natural moral law has a long honored tradition in the history of ethical theory and practice. An extended chapter is devoted to its development and some current criticisms of it. Therefore, it is not considered extensively at this point. Natural law is often appealed to as an alternative to divine revelation or biblical ethics. The appeal is to nature or to reason or to both at once.

Natural moral law theories considered historically distinguish sharply the law of nature (*jus naturale*) from the law of nations (*jus gentium*) and from civil law (*jus civile*). The last of these is enacted legislation; the first two are regarded as given in a more general sense. They are often combined with each other. Varieties of natural moral law are analyzable into differing meanings of nature. Ten or more such meanings can be differentiated. These theories can also be differentiated according to the meaning of the term "law" which is employed. A half dozen or more such meanings can be noted by careful analysis. It would follow from this that the range of natural moral law theories is very great, depending on the meaning of nature and the meaning of law which each embodies. There are, in addition, nuances which reflect several notions of nature and of law.

Some expressions of natural moral law are, in fact, fused or mixed with prescriptive moral law of various types—theological, ecclesiastical, or cultural. Sometimes in the form of a "relative" natural law these expressions might better be called "middle axioms." Such "middle axioms" will be noted elsewhere in this discussion. The relation of the moral law represented by this study to natural moral law will become evident in due course. Paul Ramsey is among the contemporary ethicists who protest against blurring the distinctions between Christian ethics and natural law ethics. He recognizes that the latter might form an important part of a completed edifice of Christian ethics.[1]

A third type of moral law presents one or more values as ultimate norms or demands. Ideal norms which have served as such ultimate moral demands are truth, justice, and love. These may be regarded as independent or as interpenetrating moral laws. They may be stated as self-evident or as divine commands. As an inclusive moral concept (*Inbegriff*) such moral law may be formulated in terms of humanity or of personality. Theologians in presenting the law of God as a law of truth, of righteousness, or of love may regard each as a definition of his nature, or a command of his will, or as an expression of his energizing.

The appeals to love, to righteousness, and to truth are sometimes stated in ways that deprecate law and even abandon it entirely. The conflicts between these ideals or norms and moral law are often due to an issue regarding prescription, i.e., codes of morality, or to questions of motives of conduct, or to questions of power to fulfill demands.

Moral law is frequently stated in terms that embody common human needs or universal themes and relationships. As distinguished from moral codes these principles are general guidelines of conduct like the Golden Rule. Not all such laws are on the same level of universality. Therefore, some command obedience in most situations unless overruled by a higher law in the hierarchy of generality. Conversely, if the highest law—the law of love —is appealed to, subordinate moral laws may also be required in order to relate it relevantly to complex concrete situations. This type of problem evokes the attempt to expound a system of moral laws which will be adequate for all situations, avoiding both abstract idealism and code prescription.

The types of moral law which have thus far been considered do not exhaust the list of modern theories. Kant's categorical imperative, for example, is a formal law emphasizing rational, autonomous, and universal volition: "act only according to that maxim by which you can at the same time will that it should become a universal law." Although Kant defended this principle as a pure principle of will, nevertheless, he presupposed substantive elements and drew axiological (value) conclusions. A concept of the good was contextually involved because he held that the categorical imperative was the criterion of the good will. He also reformulated it to say: "act so as to treat humanity, whether in your own person or in that of another, always as an end and never as a means only." The concept of humanity as an end in itself goes far beyond the pure formal law of universal rational autonomy in willing. Moreover, the manner in which Kant readily applied and argued the issues of truth telling shows that substantive issues were latent in his basic argumentation. The truth in Kant's formalism needs, nevertheless, to be incorporated into any complete consideration of moral laws.

The categorical imperative leads to other kinds of moral law reflection, such as is implied in the dictum "I ought, therefore, I can." It seeks to avoid both ethical irrelevance and moral relativism. Both irrelevance and relativism point to the need for a critical axiology, i.e., to moral laws of value. This is referred to as the problem of the good. On the one hand is a quest not to get lost in norms which cannot be applied effectively; on the other hand is the quest not to be lost in the variables of different situations. This discussion will show how the formal law of autonomy conserves what is defensible in Kant's categorical imperative and also what axiological laws are required to deal effectively with the whole range of values in the moral life.

B. REJECTIONS OF MORAL LAW

At this point we must recognize that moral law in all the senses used above is unacceptable to some Christian ethicists like Barth and Lehmann. Barth and Lehmann would agree that ethics is systematic reflection on what is involved in the ethical nature of the Christian religion.[2] Barth says, "Ethics must be understood as the attempt, scientific or otherwise, to cope with the question of good and evil in human behavior."[3] Neither Barth nor Lehmann makes ethics prescriptive, yet both reject moral philosophy. Both base ethics on what, according to the gospel, God is doing in the world. Since both these thinkers stand in contrast to the moral law theories thus far noted and the major theory to be developed in this book, it is useful to note their perspectives more fully and to indicate the points of difference in a preliminary way here.

Barth states that ethics on his assumptions can only be evangelical ethics. "The question of good and evil is never answered by man's pointing to the authoritative Word of God in terms of a set of rules. It is never discovered by man or imposed on the self and others as a code of good and evil actions, a sort of yardstick of what is good and evil."[4] Although Barth holds that ethics is a theory of human behavior, nevertheless he argues that "the grace of God protests against every humanly established ethic as such. The protest, however, is positive: grace not only negates man but still more affirms man by pursuing the solution of the ethical problem which grace provides in active refutation, resolution and suspension of all human answers to that problem."[5] God is always in encounter with man's freedom. The free God confronts free man who chooses, decides, and determines himself as a consequence of the nature of his God-given freedom. God wants man "to be His creature, His partner, and His child. What this means for each of us here and there, today and tomorrow, is decided by the free word of the free Lord in *ever renewed encounter between God and an individual*."[6] Barth rejects the notion that ethical theory should provide man with a program which would serve as life's goal and the further notion that it should present man with principles to be interpreted, applied, and put into practice. "Ethics," he says, "has to make clear that every single step man takes involves a specific and direct responsibility toward God, who reached out for man in specific and direct encounter . . . The ethos of the ethicist implies that he refrain from attempting too much and becoming thereby a lawmaker."[7] In this argument Barth does not indicate the criteria by which the Christian responsibly exercises his obedience to the God he encounters in concrete situations. Is there a system of moral laws which can supply this gap between God's nonprescriptive Word and man's particularized response? In dealing with concrete problems and evaluating the conduct of Christian groups Barth continually employs latent laws which are not manifestly acknowledged.

Lehmann also rejects moral laws and moral philosophy and does so in the interest of a *"koinonia* ethic." "A *koinonia* ethic," he argues, "ventures the claim that it has a clearer view of ethical reality as concrete human reality, and thus also of what God is doing and of what man is to do, than is offered by an ethic of principles and middle axioms."[8] This claim while stressing the contextual character of *koinonia* ethics, does not derive the context of action only from the situation, but insists that the situation is ethically significant because of what God is doing in the world.[9] Christian ethics, for Lehmann, is reflection upon the question and its answer: "What am I, as a believer in Jesus Christ and as a member of His Church, to do?"[10] This ethic he characterizes as *indicative* in contrast to *imperative* ethics. The ethical question therefore is not "What *ought* I to do?" but "What *am* I to do?" "The primary ethical reality is the human factor, the *human* indicative, in every situation involving the interrelationships and the decisions of men."[11] There are many similarities between the ethical theories of Barth and Lehmann, but this stress on the primacy of the indicative sharply differentiates them. If *ought* is reducible finally to *is* and if the *good* is rejected in favor of the *mature* (as in Lehmann), then, of course, there are no moral laws. However, it is not difficult to show that norms, goals, and imperatives are latent and even explicit at all levels of Lehmann's ethical theory. Critical value judgments are made at many points with implicit appeals to the moral laws which are explicit in the theory to be expounded.

The theories of Barth and Lehmann converge in their contextual relation to the Christian church and in their appeal to humanity. Both are explicit in such references. Lehmann says that "the will of God is the quite concrete and dynamic action of God in the world to make and keep human life human."[12] Barth says, in correcting his earlier emphasis of deity as "wholly other," the real point is God's sovereign togetherness with man. "Who God is and what He is in His deity He proves and reveals not in a vacuum as a divine being-for-Himself, but precisely and authentically in the fact that He exists, speaks, and acts as the *partner* of man."[13] This is a christological statement. "Jesus Christ is in His one Person, as true *God, man's* loyal partner, and as true *man,* God's."[14]

Just as the Kantian type of moral law raises questions about formal or logical laws in ethics, and just as the problems of the good and of values raise questions about axiological laws, so the problems of human life as a whole and of humanity in Barth and Lehmann raise questions about the moral laws of personality and community. These four levels of moral law will provide the systematic order for the idea of moral law developed in this book. When Christian ethicists affirm God's active concern for men and for humanity they inevitably become involved in types of moral judgment involving formal, axiological, personalistic, and communitarian aspects of responsibility—the four levels of law described below.

How can responsible moral choices be discriminatingly and relevantly made? Such choices involve consistency, appeal to levels of value, to consequences, to individuality and community, to ideal control, to the best possible, to autonomy, to compromise, to the specific situation, to personality growth and development, and so on. Corresponding to these ideas are possible moral laws which *ought* to be obeyed. These may well be ultimately located not only in human will and reason, in personality taken as a moral and coherent whole, but also in the context of God, but it is doubtful whether apart from loyalty to such moral laws the will of God for and in man can be discerned and done. When an all-inclusive value or norm like love is employed, such a category to be coherent must include the above referent points and component elements.

It can be shown that within the *indicative* framework of what Lehmann alleges God *is* doing in the world to make and to keep human life human there are many claims of *ought*. There is, for example, the component of autonomy which is accented within his theonomous conception of freedom. Conscience involves free obedience and wholeness. There is also the axiological component with knowledge of good and evil.[15] Lehmann takes account of consequences in making evaluations.[16] He recognizes the norm of the best possible[17] and employs the principle of ideal control. What is required, Lehmann argues, "is a context for conscience which conjoins the focus of divine activity and the focus of human responsiveness in such a way as to provide behavior with direction and decisiveness."[18] Nevertheless, he means to reject the law of consequences by substituting *insight* for *calculation* and *faith* for the *good*. "In the *koinonia* each individual, in the midst of the full complexity of all the factors involved, makes a behavioral decision which amounts, in fact, to taking in trust the risk of trust."[19] His appeal to situations and to context is analogous to what in this book is called the "law of specification."

In contrast and opposition to ethicists who try to fit cases into previous or prescriptive moral laws, Lehmann stresses the transforming power of a concrete exception and cites from the New Testament the man healed on the Sabbath day, the woman taken in adultery, the "Good Samaritan," and the "Prodigal Son" as vivid instances of the way Christianity specializes in the exception. He is not referring to exceptions which prove the rule, but to ones that suspend the rule and break new ethical ground. "Transvaluation means that the ethical inadequacy of accepted norms and values has been exposed by ethical insights and directives integrally related to the concrete ground of decision."[20] To this we may respond, Very good! Yet a question must be pressed. Does not the new insight claim to have general significance? Does it not belong to subsequent knowledge about what God is doing in the world? In *all* the world, not just in the *koinonia* of the Christian church? Does not the way the concrete situations were handled by Jesus give attitudinal guidance by redefining a norm which is relevant to a whole range of other situations? A new ethical generalization, attitude, motive, or insightful norm has become part of subsequent ethical judgment: "Go do thou likewise."

On these issues Barth seems to have grasped the universal implications of humanity in Jesus Christ more radically than Lehmann has expounded them, for Barth is not confined by the *koinonia* of the church. "On the basis of the eternal will of God we have to think of *every human being,* even the oddest, most villainous or miserable, as one to whom Jesus Christ is Brother and God is Father; and we have to deal with him on this assumption. . . . On the basis of the knowledge of the humanity of God no other attitude to any kind of fellow man is possible. It is identical with the practical acknowledgment of his human rights and his human dignity."[21] By arguing in this way Barth lays the foundation for a common ground morality that cuts across faith lines and all cultural lines. This emphasis radically corrects the exaggerations of his earlier theological position which stressed the eternal qualitative difference between time and eternity.

From the standpoint of the present writer one of the most successful efforts at presenting the Christian category of love coherently with an understanding of the elements making up discriminating judgments is that by Joseph Fletcher.[22] A presentation and brief evaluation of six propositions which he regards as the fundamentals of Christian conscience will serve to clarify a number of issues relating moral laws to Christian ethics. For Fletcher the category of love, *agape,* is the primordial or axiomatic value. This *summum bonum* cannot be reached except by an act of faith. Christian moral judgments are *decisions,* not conclusions; science and logic are only auxiliary to evaluation and choice.

The six propositions are as follows: (1) "Only one thing is intrinsically good, namely, love: nothing else." (2) "The ultimate norm of Christian decisions is love: nothing else." (3) "Love and justice are the same, for justice is love distributed." (4) "Love wills the neighbor's good whether we like him or not." (5) "Only the end justifies the means: nothing else." (6) "Decisions ought to be made situationally, not prescriptively."

In commenting on these propositions we must note how the meaning of each one and all of them together embody laws which will be systematically detailed in later chapters. First of all, Fletcher argues that values exist only in response to persons.[23] Value is not an absolute, independent existence but is always "value for a person." He approvingly quotes Brightman that "in personality is the only true intrinsic value we know or could conceive; all values are but forms of personal experience."[24] Love is "good will at work in partnership with reason, seeking the neighbor's good radically, non-preferentially."[25] Augustine was right in reducing the whole Christian ethic to the single maxim: "love and *then* what you will do," not, however, "love and do what you please!"[26] This principle is too radical to be a prescriptive legalism; it shares its power with no other kinds of law, natural or supernatural. It is, thus, the ultimate ideal which controls all other values and choices.

The category of love so interpreted contains an axiological law which commands a critical use of reason in relation to ideals like justice and the "more or less" which is relevant to concrete situations. Since justice is love distributed, it requires a consideration of the claims of self and those of the plurality of "neighbors." So conceived justice and love are not (as in Brunner and Niebuhr, says Fletcher) independent categories. In seeking social policy love acknowledges both person and community and the reshaping of subordinate principles. "Justice," Fletcher argues, "is Christian love using its head—calculating its duties."[27] It is attitudinal, not emotional. It is volitional, conative.[28] It considers consequences and makes preferential judgments. When Fletcher says that "love's method is particularity,"[29] he is affirming in effect a "law of specification." Love includes the laws of concrete moral responsibility.

The situationism of Fletcher is marked off from that of Lehmann in the following strategic formula: *"the indicative plus the imperative equals the normative.* What is, in the light of what love demands, shows what ought to be."[30]

Though oriented by faith in theological decision Barth, Lehmann, and Fletcher proceed differently in handling concrete decisions. Of the three contextualists or situationists Fletcher shows the greatest understanding of the place of the empirical in moral judgments. The relation of theological to philosophical and scientific disciplines involved in the above theories and their implications for moral law requires further analysis than the exposition has thus far provided.

We must, therefore, ask more precisely about the nature of

Christian social ethics. Following this preliminary definition, we shall trace some empirical and philosophical criticisms of the relation of person to community. Then we shall stress the ethical predicament of man, noting some theological as well as philosophical considerations. Following this, the distinctive elements of the Christian ethic will be noted, and a system of moral laws will be presented. This system, first worked out by E. S. Brightman,[31] provides an alternative to classical natural law theory and supplies the normative structure required in all Christian ethics regardless of supplementary or contextual factors. Finally, the ethical significance of Jesus Christ will be discussed.

C. NATURE OF CHRISTIAN SOCIAL ETHICS

Christian social ethics is an interdisciplinary field and therefore is difficult to define precisely. Its component disciplines are all in the process of active development and reinterpretation. Negatively speaking, Christian social ethics is not theological ethics with applications to current social questions made apart from philosophical and scientific analysis. It is not—even when the problems discussed are social—a presentation of general theoretical ethics with biblical sanctions. It is not sociology of religion or any other behavioral science. It is, positively stated, interdisciplinary, which commits its practitioners to undertake joint, supplementary, or complementary theoretical and empirical studies in theology, philosophical ethics, behavioral and historical sciences. Christian social ethics seeks emergent coherence.

Most works in Christian ethics belong either in biblical theology or systematic theology. Such books are often perceptive in regard to social questions, but this alone does not qualify them in the field of social ethics, for to so qualify they must also exhibit a knowledge of the sciences specifically relevant to empirical and situational mastery of a problem. A qualified Christian social ethicist ought to be well grounded in Bible and theology, in philosophy, in history, and in the behavioral sciences. Science, philosophy, and theology interpenetrate and converge in the methods of social ethics.

As men devise social policy, make regulations, enact legislation, they need to relate coherently their ultimate beliefs, their philosophical principles, and the requirements of persons in actual situations. These factors interpenetrate and mutually influence each other. The development of various traditions including natural law and contextual ethics reflects such interaction. As in culture as a whole so in ethical matters changes in one basic institution or segment of society effect changes in the others to some degree. New movements in philosophy such as existentialism and phenomenology tend to influence both theology and the social sciences. New movements in theology have analogous consequences though not always to the same degree. Similarly new developments in the behavioral sciences—including such concepts as culture referred to above—influence both philosophical and theological thought. The quality and degree of influence, we may suggest, depend in part on how closely initiating changes are related to the central values of a culture.

Christian social ethics should take note of the significance of central cultural values. Talcott Parsons, sociologist, considers religion as a phenomenon which relates, and thus in a sense integrates, three subsystems—cultural systems, personality systems, and social systems.[32] Religion is understood here as that which is rooted in the most generalized orientations of meaning. Though religion has this basic function of integration, theology needs social science to come to terms with it. Parsons feels that theology as such is not able to provide the functional differentiation which sociology makes possible. Science helps theology to be more sophisticated because it can then be more precise about the way its phenomena and data function. It helps theology to be relationally more self-aware.

If theology teaches people to care because God cares, anthropology can teach theology much on how to care in areas of rapid social change because, as Margaret Mead says, the "systematic or patterned quality of culture is a function of the integrated character of human beings, who, as they incorporate cultural traits, sometimes very diverse in origin, organize them into viable ways of life."[33] Chief Justice Earl Warren in an appeal for the development of counselors of social ethics has argued that law cannot exist without ethics. "In civilized life, law floats in a sea of ethics. Each is indispensable to civilization. Without law, we should be at the mercy of the least scrupulous; without ethics law could not exist."[34] Today mankind is the unit of co-operation. Within that unity there is both purposeful and un-purposed co-operation. From the interaction of persons, groups, and institutions a world civilization that is predominantly scien-tific, technical, and urban is emerging. World civilization re-quires world law, and world law requires world ethics. A merely private ethics with only contexts of private situations is not seri-ously thinkable. World ethics requires an ethos, a myth-struc-ture, a self-enforcing complex of meanings and values to hold such a society together. Moral law must be relevant to global responsibility.

It is often acknowledged that law cannot evoke a nonexistent ethic or one that has become uncouth, obsolete, or irrelevant. Scientific validity and moral propriety must be sought together and reconciled through the worth of persons. It is persons who must make the transition from one cultural stage to the next. "In all technical change," writes Margaret Mead, "even when it seems to be concerned with tools, machines and other imper-sonal objects, the individual person is both the recipient of change and the mediator or agent of change. His integrity as a person, his stability as a personality, must be kept ever in focus as the living concern of all purposive change."[35]

What sort of creature, then, is man? How is person re-lated to community? What bearing do philosophical and sci-entific thinking have on moral law which does justice to per-sons in community? It is one of the theses of this book that if the contextual ethic of a Barth, a Lehmann, or a Fletcher is to be concretely relevant to decisions, it must be aware of all the empirical aspects of these situations and must be corrected and disciplined by moral laws which command the person to choose coherently at the logical, the axiological, the personalistic, and the communitarian levels.

II
PERSON AND COMMUNITY

The relation of persons to social wholes is one of the most fascinating problems of modern science and philosophy, as it is one of the most important in practical ethics. In this chapter we shall deal with basic philosophical and scientific issues, illustrating them from the history of ideas since Leibniz and relating them to a personalistic hypothesis which we may designate as communitarian. The reality of social wholes and the relation of persons to social wholes and each other constitute the general problem of our inquiry. We shall explore our attempted definitions through the following four steps of discussion: (a) person and community in certain modern philosophers; (b) person and community in historical wholes; (c) person and community in sociological theory; and (d) the nature of community as an organic pluralism.

A. PERSON AND COMMUNITY IN MODERN IDEALISM

As a background we may note some of the social conceptions of Leibniz, Hegel, Lotze, Troeltsch, Royce, Hocking, and Brightman. This procedure is adopted because personalists take the historical community of philosophical criticism seriously as an aid to precise definition and coherence of conception. Pluralism is the historical starting point for the discussion.

Leibniz, like Lotze and Brightman, conceived of ultimate reality as a divine society. The assembly of all spirits constitutes the City of God which may also be called a universal monarchy. Each spirit is an active, purposive center, a monad, which reflects the whole universe as a living mirror and is itself an image of Divinity. By a pre-established harmony God has established the order of monads into the best of all possible worlds.

The evils which they commit are ultimately due to their finitude. Their relations to each other are only through God, for
the monads have no windows. They have no genuine interaction. The social order is not really interpersonal. There is
nothing but privacy internally governed by the Absolute Mon-
arch of the Universe. No genuine communion enhances the
harmony of the active spirits. "God produces different substances
according to the different views which he has of the world, and by
the intervention of God, the appropriate nature of each substance brings it about that what happens to one corresponds to
what happens to all the others, without, however, their acting
upon one another directly."[1] Leibniz's plenum is an assembly of
active monads pluralistic in the extreme, except for the Supreme
Monad.

Hegel, on the other hand, as commonly understood, presents
a conception of the whole which threatens to destroy the
integrity of the individual person. Absolute idealism stresses the
ultimate whole at the expense of finite wholes. Hegel intended, however, to champion the full actualization of personality in his philosophy, even in the period of his devotion to
the Prussian state. Tsanoff writes quite properly: "Conscious as
he increasingly became of the paramount importance of social
order and institutional structure, he never wavered in his emphasis on the self-realization of personality. No one in modern
philosophy, while recognizing the clefts and contradictions in
life, set himself more resolutely to express the prevailing principles
of integrity and concrete unity."[2]

Hegel's awareness of the concrete social whole surcharged with
the tensional dynamics of subordinate spiritual creativity is expressed in the idea of dialectic. This dialectic finally includes, as
it compels thought to recognize, the Absolute. Our concern here,
however, is not with the Absolute but with the person in relation
to social wholes. Persons are actualized only in larger wholes.
There is a dimension of subjectivity in man and hence in morals,
but this is only one moment in the whole, for there is in man
a will which seeks universality and which objectifies itself in institutions. The self is, to be sure, subjectively free as viewed at one

stage of the dialectic, but it is compelled by the dialectic of self-actualization to objective participation in community with other selves in more concrete freedom. Hegel begins with abstract right (the Kantian formal autonomy) and then proceeds to a consideration of morality which views the objective laws which the self obeys as free self-identification. He then progresses to the ethical system of social institutions, such as the fulfillment of man in the family, in the life of citizenship on the level of work and business, and finally in the state as the highest educator of character. "The state is the Divine Idea as it exists on earth." As a member of the state, man realizes his highest ethical goal.

At the level of man's relation to the state, Hegel seems to subordinate the individual to the will of a reified objective spirit. The point is much in dispute. Hegel's own words are open to more than one interpretation. On the one hand, the dialectic seems to carry the conception of personality to ever higher levels of social actualization; on the other hand, Hegel seems to have taught that Objective Mind is a self-conscious subject. It is instructive that both Rousseau and Hegel stress the passionate freedom of the individual and also the objective reality of the General Will and the state. Neither of them had a sufficiently clear understanding of the distinction between the community and the state; neither of them realized sufficiently that the state is an association and not an organic social whole which includes all other social wholes; neither of them had a sufficiently pluralistic conception of personality-in-community.

In the philosophy of Lotze, the relation of the person to social reality moves again in the direction of Leibniz. But Lotze's monadism does not go the extreme individualistic lengths of Leibniz. The all-pervading and all-embracing Divine Personality is conceived in a thoroughly spiritual metaphysics, but the active centers of being, though self-identical, genuinely interact and constitute an infinite variety of modes of co-operation. The real interaction of monads is the basis on which Lotze builds his proof of the existence of God. Lotze developed an argument—which was elaborated further in the thought of Bowne—that the fact of interaction according to laws ought to lead us to believe in the necessary unity of the substance underlying the world and, moreover, that this can only be properly conceived as personality, as self-conscious spirit. Interpersonal interaction became also a hallmark of American personalism.

In Lotze's view of cosmic society a very high place is given to the experience of value. Value is not merely subjective, but must be understood in terms of the teleology of nature which is both immanent and integral. Values are hierarchically evaluated. Man's appreciation of value is higher on the scale as it expresses wholeness of personality. Love is the ultimate value in the Divine Personality, the cosmos being a divinely ordered instrumentality for the achievement of spiritual character and its worth.[1]

Lotze had a determinative influence on Troeltsch. Although in all idealism the creative activity of thought and will makes for a conception of personality as initiating agent, Troeltsch nevertheless was profoundly impressed by the phenomenon of historical wholes within the process of history. We shall note below how his historical totalities give to culture a unity without, however, falling into monistic interpretations of social causation. He avoided the Hegelian reification of ethical ideals in culture and history as successive dialectical expressions of ethical ideals. He saw the problem of relativism in all cultural and historical inquiry quite clearly: "If one starts out from Ideas and standards one falls into an unhistorical rationalism and loses contact with empirical history and its practice. If one starts out from the historical-individual and thereby remains in harmony with research, a limitless relativism and scepticism threaten one. If one attempts to come close to both through ingenious concepts of development the two aspects always break asunder."[4] He saw that "the concrete situation demands concrete standards."[5] In his studies the problem of the cultural historian and the axiologist comes to the fore: how any historical event or value can claim universal validity.[6] No more acute problem faces the student of culture who envisages the practical issues of creating one world. The wholistic reality of historical totalities was given a marked pluralistic emphasis in Troeltsch.

In Royce the emphasis is more Hegelian. Absolute idealism finally dominates over the personalistic or pluralistic elements in his social theory. Royce believed in freedom, however, holding that in free acts man is the Absolute in action and that nothing else in the Absolute determines the nature of the act. The role of community was emphasized by him in terms both of knowledge and of ethics. Knowledge is social. The world is a self-interpreting community of individuals. "In the concrete . . . the universe is a community of interpretation whose life comprises and unifies all the social varieties and all the social communities which, for any reason, we know to be real in the empirical world which our social and our historical sciences study. The history of the universe, the whole order of time, is the history and the order and the expression of this Universal Community."[7] Royce's ethics centered in the principle of "loyalty," man's devotion to a "cause" greater than himself. His ultimate moral principle was "loyalty to loyalty" which means that the individual respects and co-operates with the spirit of loyalty wherever he finds it. This was his approach to international and also to ultimate religious questions.

The idealism of W. E. Hocking conceives the relation of person to community within a monistic metaphysics but with a pluralistic psychology. Social groups are real as vital "will circuits," but they are not transcendental realities as in Hegel. For example in a state the "wills of the citizens constitute a genuine unity without fusing into a mystical and inoperable corporate personality."[8] "The individual," he points out, "is prior to the state," but "the state is prior to the complete individual. He needs the state to become the person that he has it in him to become."[9]

Hocking accepts the doctrine of natural human sociability in which there inheres simple animal gregariousness.[10] This gregariousness is entangled with all sorts of other human traits and is itself but an instinctive rudiment, a "spark that starts the motor." Sociability is really mental and involves judgment and value levels. The self is not a product of society. "We depend on society for self-measurement, not for self-consciousness, not for the raw material of our ideals, certainly not for selfhood."[11] Judgment, for example, must be one's own or it is not judgment, and one who merely repeats or adapts it is so far not a mind. Similarly, conscience is not basically a social product. "Unless conscience is my own, it is not conscience." The same argument holds for the idea of self-consciousness. Self-consciousness, he affirms, is present from the beginning of selfhood. "Unless the self is something without society, it can be nothing with it. If, when I think, it is society that thinks in me, there is no thought, and no society."[12]

Although emphasizing the reality of individual selves, Hocking recognizes the difficulties of social atomism.[13] He notes that groups have mental qualities which do not appear to be derived from the qualities of unit-members. The well-bounded monad would make mutual understanding impossible, for it would be shut off from the beginning. In some sense groups are organisms, but they are not super-minds.[14] The conception which Hocking proposes is the "will-circuit." Since selves are not self-sufficient monads, they need extensions of will and habit which complete the circuit through the common sharing of external objects. The participants in a "will-circuit" have lives of their own, but the circuit may often seem to approach autonomy. It makes a claim to live, for it is a living thing, not a mere abstraction or fiction. "Will-circuits" have individuality, but they are not selves. "The only selves present are those of the participants or members."[15]

In the personalism of Brightman, the social character of reality at all levels is made an explicit principle. He views "all reality as a society of selves or persons, with a cosmic person as its central, vivifying, creative force." "The personalist thinks of a person as a complex, but unified and self-identifying self-experience; and the human personality is viewed as being in constant interaction and communication with the rest of the personal universe."[16] Everything that we call "impersonal" is really an aspect of personal reality. Brightman's metaphysics is to be distinguished from Hegel's and Royce's in being quantitatively pluralistic while theirs is monistic. Therefore the view that the universe is a society of many communicating and interacting persons and selves is to be sharply distinguished from the view which conceives of reality as a single self containing the many as its parts.[17]

Few thinkers have been so explicit in relating their ideas to earlier philosophy or in constant redefinition as Brightman. He points out that the pluralism is asserted, in part, because "social relations, and especially the relations of love and cooperation between person and person, lose their meaning when personal distinctness is denied and all persons melt into one." This is important too with respect to the axiological goal of personalism: "reason and love, or coherent love. In a society of persons, creative cooperation, mutual respect, loving devotion to truth, and the highest possible attainment of the experience of God, constitute the purposive substance of metaphysical reality."[18]

Persons are in continual interaction with each other, whether known or not. Persons initiate causes and suffer effects.[19] Interpersonal interaction to be meaningful requires interpersonal communication. In one sense each person " 'prehends' all humanity." Communication leads to action, either of co-operation or conflict. Brightman summarizes the levels of interpersonal relations as follows: "(1) the level of mere causation—receptivity or action without awareness of the other persons affecting us or being affected by us; (2) the level of sympathy and antipathy—liking or disliking what others communicate to us; (3) the level of understanding—where the person or group is properly interpreted, yet perhaps all the more disliked; and (4) the level of love."[20] "The ultimate category is social; the goal of the universe is inexhaustible, developing love" which presupposes and rationally criticizes all lower levels of interpersonal interaction.[21] In concrete terms this means a social view which may be called "social personalism or democratic socialism."

B. PERSON AND COMMUNITY IN HISTORICAL WHOLES

Personalists tend to adopt an organic pluralism not only in general metaphysics but also in their approach to historical wholes. What light does the interpretation of history throw on the understanding of the person-in-community? We have noted Hegel's conception of social wholes in the form of objective spirit and the state. Ultimately the dialectic of thought and of process presented him with but one whole, the Absolute Idea. The conception of social wholes may be regarded as a permanent Hegelian contribution to philosophy, but how shall they be understood? Even when Marx sought to set the Hegelian dialectic on its head he did not repudiate the organic principle of social wholes in historical interpretation. He rejected *the* whole but not social wholes. Neither did he reject the role of persons in history. In the "Eleven Theses Against Feuerbach," for example, Marx accepted the principle of creative activity of persons in interaction with historical process. Though he conceived of historical wholes in terms which seem to exaggerate the economic aspects of society, he did not conceive ideas or human action as the mere reflection of impersonal technological or economic forces. "The chief defect of all previous materialism," writes Marx, "is that the object, reality, sensibility, is conceived only in the form of the object or as conception, but not as human sensory activity, practice (Praxis), not subjectively. . . . Feuerbach . . . does not conceive human activity itself as an objective activity."[22]

Marx's philosophy has led many thinkers and a whole movement into conceiving of society in class terms to the disadvantage of the person. Yet it is dubious whether this charge is properly leveled against his own interpretation of the situation. Marx's understanding of dialectic led him to repudiate the religious absolute, the conception of history as the autobiography of God, and philosophy as retrospective evaluation; it led him to combat social atomism and abstract ethical idealism; it led him to affirm process, human purpose, social wholes, and consciousness as an integral part of the social process. "The proletariat," he writes, "senses in its position in society its own destruction, becomes aware of the character of its inhuman existence and of its own helplessness. . . . Private property abolishes itself only in so far as it produces the proletariat *as* a proletariat, whose physical and spiritual misery becomes conscious misery, and which in becoming conscious of its inhuman condition succeeds in abolishing it."[23] Thus, while Marx repudiated idealism as a philosophy, he retained in his conception of the person's relation to society the idealistic doctrine of the creative activity of thought and the strong voluntarism of Kant and Hegel. The synoptic method of viewing historical

wholes dialectically protects theory from monocausal explanations. We shall note below that this idea, so important to personalism, is being felt in some contemporary social psychology as well. Marx's words are explicit: "The materialistic doctrine that men are the products of other circumstances and education, and that changed men are therefore the products of other circumstances and a changed education, forgets that circumstances are changed by men, and that the educator must himself be educated. . . . The coincidence of the transformation of circumstances and of human activity can only be conceived and rationally understood as revolutionizing practice."[24]

The appreciation of social wholes and the creative participation of persons is found in a marked degree also in the work of Ernst Troeltsch[25] and John Elof Boodin.[26] Troeltsch's fundamental historical category, noted above, is the Individual Totality. In history we find *wholes* which are syntheses of psychical process and natural conditions. Each constitutes a life unity or totality. Typical totalities are the family, class, folk, state, cultural epoch, religious community, revolution, war, or a school of thought. Such social wholes have five essential characteristics: (1) common spirit or mind, (2) originality and unrepeatableness, (3) unity of meaning and value, (4) the unconscious, and (5) creativity and freedom.

In dealing with the category of common spirit, Troeltsch wished to avoid two fallacies: the first would explain common spirit as a mere collection or product of previously isolated individual consciousnesses which come into accidental intercourse with each other; the second would explain common spirit as a mystical entity abstracted from all individual consciousness. Nevertheless, common spirit is objectively real; it is a primary phenomenon (*ein Urphänomen*). Troeltsch conceived that individual men participate in plural common spirits, many of them like concentric or intersecting circles each with its own ethical spirit. From this historical situation arise some of our most serious moral predicaments and the problem of the relativity of all norms, for the same person participates in social wholes having contrary value structures. The relation may be not conflict but subordination. There are also larger unities of meaning and value which may include the lesser as in, for example, the spirit of the Middle Ages.

Troeltsch held to plural historical causality within and among historical wholes, including the interactions with the nonhuman environment. He recognized the unity of meaning and value and the problem of how individual meanings are related to whole meanings. But he did not carry the conception as far along this line as is necessary. The creativity and spontaneity of the individual person in the Individual Totality is constantly affirmed. History is to a degree unpredictable, and any thought of universal law, either naturalistic or dialectic, is impossible. Though Troeltsch appreciated Marx and the economic interpretation of history as making a great contribution to the study of Individual Totalities, he stressed the primordial depths and autonomy of creativity and the unpredictable originality of men like Jesus, Paul, Luther, Napoleon, and Marx. This he grounded in a spiritual metaphysics.

Boodin went beyond Troeltsch. He employed the very controversial term "the Social Mind." In his essay "The Existence of Social Minds," he postulated intersubjective continuity as an elementary fact. By intersubjective continuity he meant "the immediate consciousness of mental responsiveness." Minds, like matter, he conceived as existing in fields with their own continuities and with their own interplay of parts. In the psychical field we respond immediately to the character and intensity of mind. We recognize other minds within the field immediately and intuitively. This intuition is not knowledge, but it precedes theory. Conative responsiveness is unique. The intersubjective continuum is implied, he said, in all intercourse of minds; it is a creative synthesis, a real emergent in the dynamic process of nature.

The question persists: are there Social Minds and of what order of reality are they? Boodin held that the Social Mind is a mind because it is a begetter of personality, because it is begotten synthetically from mind, because it acts empirically like a mind, and because of intuitive awareness of intersubjective continuity. Boodin emphasized mind as a gestalt of energy, i.e., of will; conation and volition are basic. In his definition of mind, consciousness is subordinate to energy. The Social Mind itself is purposive; indeed, purpose is a basic category of social reality.

There are four characteristics which individual minds possess in common with Social Minds: fusion, quality, intensity, and number. *Fusion* refers to the unifying of complex factors; *quality* refers to the fact of variety of kinds of factors in the fusion. *Intensity* refers to the degree of fusion; and *number* refers to the quantity of component factors involved. A Social Mind so composed is a genuine subject, Boodin argued, because it is uniquely selective and may be creative in a social situation. It is temporal. It has a nonconscious substratum made up of traditions, customs, and mores. It may exhibit loyalty and other moral traits. Like the personal mind, the Social Mind may suffer pathologically: hysteria, paranoia, mania, delusions of grandeur, depressions, fixed ideas, and other maladies may afflict it.

Boodin seemed to hold that intersubjective continuity is substantive, as if there were in Social Mind a real compounding of will and consciousness. "Our minds are confluent, even physically or metaphysically. . . . we are really members of one another." If there is a real fusion of wills in a substantive Social Mind, we may ask, on the one hand, how the integrity of the individual person is conserved and what becomes of the consciousness of genuine privacy. On the other hand, there seems to be a second conception of intersubjective continuity in Boodin which affirms that wills are fused in the sense of participating in common meanings and that what intersect are planes of meaning as persons communicate or wills converge in common ends. Thus it would seem that social fusion is both a creative achievement of personal minds and of the group as a whole through the continuum of meaning.

To the present writer it would seem sounder to hold that there are energy fields within which persons interact and which interact with each other. Social interaction takes place at levels both below consciousness and on the level of shared meaning or communication. It may have a setting as broad as intercultural process. Meaning is selective of fields of interaction and it is also a product of interaction. But meaning apart from personality is an abstraction. Social Mind is a level of existence, as Boodin says, not above or below personal minds, but on the same metaphysical level. The consciousness of "objective spirit" is not distinct from us but exists in us. The content of social *Gestalten,* historical totalities, communities, or other wholes is too rich to be entertained immediately by any person, but it is part of a field of meaning and value participated in by many persons. No person has an immediate intuition of this total content. But the field or social whole is not a self-consciousness. It is a reality which a person objectively confronts epistemologically even while participating in it socio-psychologically. It is neither a new personal consciousness on its own level of metaphysical existence nor a self-conscious subject expressing itself through us. The individual minds participate in it; they are aware of each other in it; through it group decisions and purposes are achieved; as a *Gestalt* of minds it may act with selectivity and creativity; but it is, nevertheless, what Hocking would call a "Near-mind," not a personal subject. Meaning provides the significant level of continuity within it.

A theory of social fields is an important prerequisite for a doctrine of community because participation in social groups is so crucial a relationship. There are degrees and types of participation. The elaboration of these ideas would constitute a complete social psychology. Boodin emphasized three main types. Participation may be *automatic* where the individual accepts unquestioningly and unthinkingly the customs and beliefs of the group; participation may be *dogmatic* as in the medieval world where the participants in church authority felt no fundamental antagonism between faith and reason; or participation may be *critical* where the control is rationally objective. Critical participation has several levels, the highest of which is *creative.* Social science and philosophy today would undoubtedly add many other classifications to these. But Boodin's classifications suggest a range of situations both objective and subjective.

In philosophy of history personalists recognize that the metaphysical traits of personality are not merely the products of social forces. The quality of personal actualization depends greatly, however, on the kind of participation in social wholes which history in any period makes possible. In all persons there is a center of initiating response.

The above survey of selected writers points up a number of ideas which are significant for personalistic thought in social ethics. The problem of the person and community is illuminated by the following conceptions: (1) the creative activity of persons in interaction with historical process; (2) the reality of social wholes; (3) the fruitfulness of synoptic method as well as analysis in interpreting historical wholes dialectically; (4) the complexity of historical wholes as involving such traits as common spirit, originality and unrepeatableness, unity of meaning and value, the influence of unconscious factors, freedom, and creativity; (5) the objective reality of social wholes as interpersonal psychical entities involving will, conation, meaning, personal presence and interaction, and levels of participation; and (6) the rejection of the conception of Social Mind as a self-conscious subject. In short, historical interpretation must recognize a form of organic pluralism such as that indicated in the previous section. Personalism in relation to social philosophy is neither atomistic and individualistic, on the one hand, nor superorganic and absolutistic on the other. Persons are interdependent. They are participants in the historic drama of creating communities and the kind of normative community in which persons are truly actualized. In an understanding of community, not only historical understanding but also sociological inquiry makes an important contribution. The contributions of certain sociological theorists will now be noted.

C. PERSON AND SOCIETY IN SOCIOLOGICAL THEORY

Important contributions to the communitarian philosophy of personalism have been made in sociological and anthropological inquiry. George Herbert Mead is not a personalist, but his studies of mind, self, and society emerge in a conception of the dialectical relation of person and society which is noteworthy. His view is sometimes erroneously confused with the idea that the self is nothing but a social function. He analyzed the social genius of the self and of mind as over against traditional social science which ignored the biological level, and as over against biological individualism which ignored the social nature of the underlying biological process in which minds arise.[27] Despite his concern for the social context or field, he nevertheless maintained the importance of the participating person: "The individual is no thrall of society. He constitutes society as genuinely as society constitutes the individual."[28] Every action of the individual involving communication changes the social structure to some degree, slightly for the most part, greatly in the case of the genius and the leader.

Mentality in persons refers to the organism's pointing out meanings. Mind in this sense, Mead taught, is not intracranial but refers to the whole context of relationships and components in the social field. "Mentality resides in the ability of the organism to indicate that in the environment which answers to his response, so that he can control those responses in various ways."[29] Mind appears when the social process is brought under the experience of a participating individual and is modified and refined by the awareness or consciousness which he has of it.[30] It is by means of reflexiveness, self-conscious self-transcendence, that the whole social process is thus brought into the experience of the persons involved. Reflexiveness is the essential condition, within the social process, for the development of mind. The individual gains the mechanism of reflective thought, or the ability to direct his action in terms of the foreseen consequences of alternative courses of action, in virtue of the internalization or importation of the social process of communication.

The polarity of what Mead calls the "Me" and the "I" is significant for the understanding of the points chiefly under consideration. In his usage the "Me" represents the values of the group, that sort of experience which the group makes possible. The "Me" is thus essentially a member of a social group. Its values are the values that belong to society. They claim to be supreme and call out, under certain extreme and religious conditions, the sacrifices of the self to the whole. "Just as there could not be individual consciousness except in a social group, so the individual in a certain sense is not willing to live under certain conditions which would involve a sort of suicide of the self in its process of realization."[31] Over against the "Me" stand the values associated with the "I," those values which are found in the immediate attitude of the artist, the inventor, the scientist, etc., values which involve a reconstruction of society, and so of the "Me" also which belongs to that society. There is a self-experience that stands over against the "Me" and answers it. The "I" in action involves an adaptation which affects both the rest of the self and the environment, even while it helps to constitute the self and the social matrix.

There exists thus a dialectic, composed of a complex of component factors, which makes up the dynamic of social process. There is always a mutual relationship of the individual and the community in which the individual lives. As the individual changes, the community he affects changes, which in turn provides a different environment shaping the experience of the individual, who in turn reacts in terms of the "Me" of social values and the "I" of social creativity. Persons of great mind and great character express with power in the larger community, as leaders, what is observable in the small community group in all persons.[32] At this point Mead joins with Hegel, Marx, Troeltsch, and Boodin in recognizing the primordial character of the creative genius. The very definition of genius comes back to an incalculable quality, "this change of the environment on the part of the individual by himself becoming a member of the community."[33]

Gordon W. Allport agrees with G. H. Mead on the process whereby persons develop a sense of self, recognizing that the self in all its aspects is predominantly a social product.[34] Yet he sees the basic problem in psychology as still being the discovery of the proper balance between uniform factors and individual morphogenic factors in personality. To this end he welcomes the recent impact of such movements as existentialism, phenomenology, client-centered therapy, and so-called ego-psychology. He has championed an emphasis upon the inner organization of motives, traits, and personal style. Says Allport, "I persist in my belief that patterned individuality should be, and can be, a datum of the science of personality. This conviction leads me to resist the reduction of personality to commonalities found in all men."[35] "Psychology is *assigned* the task of being curious about human persons, and persons exist only in concrete and unique patterns."[36] This conviction of the role of psychology has philosophical and ethical implications. Man "is more than a representative of his species, more than a citizen of the state, more than an incident in the movements of mankind. He transcends them all. . . . no society holds together for long without the respect man shows to man."[37]

The sociological study of persons in social wholes has been greatly stimulated and refined by the development of field theory and group dynamics research. Many techniques have been developed in sociometry, group observation, interview techniques, and others which have been useful in studying the structural properties of groups, the relation of larger to member wholes, and the relation of social wholes to participating members. Conceptual precision has aided experimental work. As Kurt Lewin says: "The taboo against believing in the existence of a social entity is probably most effectively broken by handling this entity experimentally."[38] Field theory supports the notion of organic pluralism and cumulative multiple causation because of the versatility of its method and its integration of the social sciences. "In social research the experimenter has to take into consideration such factors as the personality of individual members, the group structure, ideology and cultural values, and economic factors. . . . Experimentation with groups . . . will force the social scientist to recognize as reality the totality of factors which determine group life."[39]

It is fruitful for our over-all conception to note the realistic way in which Lewin's field theory faces the problems of "subjective" and "objective" aspects of social fields. The prediction of group behavior, he points out, is impossible apart from a knowledge of group goals, group standards, group values, and the way a group "sees" its own situation and that of other groups. Differences in perception are crucial to understanding conflict. A three-step procedure is called for, "moving from the separate analysis of the life space of each group to the group conduct in the total social field and from there back again to the effect on the group life space."[40] This procedure of swinging from an analysis of "perception" to that of "action," from the "subjective" to the "objective" and back again, mirrors one of the basic properties of group life. Circular causal processes are at work in which fact-find depends on the way the situation is affected by action and which in turn influences or steers action.[41] A combination of "subjective" and "objective" methods seems most fruitful in studying a field situation synoptically. In this context some of the experimental work done in relating individual and group procedures to changing social conduct is important, but cannot be carried further here even briefly.[42]

Field theory such as that conducted by Lewin, his associates, and followers, the integration of psychological and sociological methods, and the co-ordination of social sciences generally have led to a growing scientific maturity on the question of the nature of cultural reality. In his study *Man and His Works,* Melville J. Herskovits concludes that culture "must never be conceived as reducing the individual to a passive or inert status in the process. Actually, the process of adjustment is circular and never-ending."[43] Culture is the instrument whereby the individual adjusts to his total setting and thereby gains the means for creative expression. Culture, nevertheless, is a whole. For purposes of study it can be broken down into traits and complexes, but "every way of life follows patterns that are integrated so as to make up a functioning whole."[44]

Any workable theory of culture needs therefore the concepts of pattern and integration. The cultural whole and the individual are realities which cannot be reduced to each other. The person, as we shall see, makes a communitarian conception possible. Though "culture can be treated as a phenomenon susceptible, through reification, of study in terms of its own structures and processes, it must be concluded that the reality of culture is psychological."[45] At the same time the very personality of the individual is to a large extent the result of his enculturative experience.[46] Like Herskovits, David Bidney holds that in the study of culture the primacy must be given to personality. It is only in a secondary sense that culture may be conceived as an impersonal, superorganic tradition comprising the aggregate of material and/or ideal products of a given society or of mankind as a whole. Says Bidney, "one reason for the confusion in contemporary culture theory is the failure on the part of social scientists to distinguish adequately between the dynamic, personal conception of culture and the static, impersonal conception involved in the notion of the cultural heritage."[47] He presses the personalistic point that "only individuals or societies can spontaneously initiate and perpetuate cultural processes which may result in superorganic cultural achievements, and hence there can be no autonomous cultural process independent of human intelligence and voluntary effort."[48]

The use of the term "individual" in sociological theory has been critically treated by Casserley. Persons, he states, have concrete and historical reality, but the individual is just a concept. "The individual is an abstraction, and possibly not even a very useful one." None of us have met any individuals for they do not exist. "At best the individual is a metaphysical concept denoting the bare possibility or potentiality of becoming personal."[49] But the term "person" is concrete and communitarian. Personality and society properly understood are not antithetical but complementary conceptions. Social science thus is bound to recognize the natural union between the person and the group. Education and ethics must proceed on the insight that man is "not by nature a complete egoist who has to be broken into social behavior against all his instincts, as an animal is trained to the yoke."[50] He achieves his prized selfhood primarily through what unites him to his fellows, not what distinguishes him, and he achieves freedom through social consciousness, not in spite of it.[51] Even the genius, the most striking case of individuality, cannot come to his fulfillment outside a society. The artist is nothing apart from his mastery of communication. Kierkegaard recognized this when he wrote: "The individual becomes conscious of himself as being this particular individual with particular gifts, tendencies, impulses, passions, under the influence of a particular environment, as a particular product of his milieu. He who becomes thus conscious of himself assumes all this as part of his own responsibility. At the moment of choice he is thus in complete isolation, for he withdraws from his surroundings; and yet he is in complete continuity, for he chooses himself as product; and this choice is a free choice, so that we might even say, when he chooses himself as product, that he is producing himself."[52]

A statement by a leading social scientist recognizes the current need to integrate individual and social approaches in social psychology.[53] T. M. Newcomb notes that psychological social theory has never really faced the implications of the psychologist's claim to study the "organism in environment." On the other hand, the sociological social theorists have never come to terms with the biological and psychological conditions under which human organisms "selectively participate in their environment. Their fallacy—if I may state it in extreme form—has been that of assuming that human organisms are virtually empty receptacles into which culture is simply poured."[54] Newcomb explores the possibilities of a social psychology which takes "full account of the realities of psychological processes as well as the realities of social organization."[55]

One of the newer conceptual outlines has to do with the importance of social norms formulated in terms of perceptual processes. Social norms represent shared ways of perceiving things, i.e., shared frames of reference within which things are perceived. Communication would seem to be a type of interaction which presupposes shared frames of reference. "The processes of norm-building and of communication are circularly related to each other. Norms arise through communication, which in turn is made possible because norms already exist."[56]

Stated in other terms what we have here is the ubiquitous problem of the anthropologists concerning the relation of cultural to psychological reality. Herskovits points out, for example, the need to define in the most precise terms the response of the individual to his total setting and the manner in which this setting conditions the individual.[57] Not dichotomy but interaction is the scientific reality. As applied to values this poses the problem of "cultural relativism." For the scientist the cultural relativistic viewpoint does not entail anarchy in values since relativism is a cross-cultural and not an intra-cultural matter. Yet, the philosophical and ethical problem persists as soon as universal claims are seriously made or denied for any norms.

The problem is more than descriptively empirical in the present period when a world community is being developed. Standards of judgment enter into so many phases of communication that the issues of personal and group norms have more than academic significance. Since all social science and the alleged validity of "cultural relativism" presuppose the primacy and dignity of the person, we have the fact of the universal claim of this value (the valuer of all values) squarely before us. Some have raised the question whether science is capable of cultural transcendence. If it is, it will be found possible because in a very real sense the person who is the bearer of all culture is always potentially a culture-transcending creative being and because the person has a value which science must (and does) presuppose. Scientific work is actually going on within the most diverse cultures.

The relation of person to community is recognized in sociological theory to be an intimate one. Although some sociologists and anthropologists tend to conceive of the person as but a function of the community or cultural whole, there are important scientific considerations in favor of an integral person-in-community conception. Certain ideas, we have noted, stand out: (1) Person and society are not antagonistic ideas but involve each other. (2) The individual (meaning the person) constitutes society as genuinely as society constitutes the individual. (3) Internal to the self is a structure (Mead's "Me") which tends to represent the values of the group, but over against it, though internal to the same self, is a self-conscious self-transcendence which makes rational creative initiative possible. (4) Even field theory, which some regard as dispensing with the creative person-in-community, recognizes a genuine dialectic of subjective and objective factors. (5) Cultural analysis as handled by certain outstanding authorities concludes that culture (a broader concept than community) in reality is psychological. That is, though culture is a whole (see "historical wholes" of the previous section) the individual (person) should not be conceived as having only a passive or inert status in the process. (6) There is need in the study of communication to examine carefully the role or function of norms. Norms influence the perception of things and the quality of interpersonal interaction. (7) This leads to a recognition of the place of values in community and the objectivity of values (norms) in cultural transcendence. (8) The possibility of transcultural norms rests on the ability of the person for self-transcendence and on the postulate of his dignity even amidst cultural relativity, for he is the valuer of all values. His worth is presupposed in all value criticism.

D. THE NATURE OF COMMUNITY

Thus far we have discussed the relation of persons to social wholes without any special reference to the concept of community. The organic pluralism which clearly emerges as the resultant from a consideration of the above philosophers and scientists is significant for any treatment of the community. But the community needs now to be explicitly, though of necessity briefly, dealt with. Community is both a descriptive and a normative term. For the purposes of this essay we shall descriptively distinguish it from association and normatively analyze it because of its value for the person. Communities are social wholes and as such must be understood in the light of the synoptic and analytical factors outlined in the sections above. In the writings of MacIver we have one of the most useful discussions of the nature of community and one which is essentially personalistic.

In *Community* Robert M. MacIver says, "By a community I mean any area of common life, village, town or district or country or even wider area."[58] Again, it is "a social unity whose members recognize as common a sufficiency of interests to allow of the interactivities of common life."[59] This latter statement may tend to confuse association and community, for it does not explicitly clarify "sufficiency of interests" and "interactivities of common life." He is clearer in *Society: Its Structure and Changes*: "Any circle of people, who live together, who belong together, so that they share, not this or that particular interest, but a whole set of interests wide enough and complete enough to include their lives, is a community."[60] In this latter definition community is not necessarily confined to a geographical area, but it is sharply differentiated from association. "An association is a group specifically organized for the pursuit of an interest or group of interests in common."[61] Men belong to associations by virtue of specific interests.

The distinction here is roughly that of Tönnies in his differentiation of *Gesellschaft* and *Gemeinschaft*. By the latter he referred to the natural, spontaneous, organic relations of people as they develop out of mutual affection, acquaintance, custom, and tradition. By *Gesellschaft* he meant the more formal contractual organization of society. A community is not a mere collection of associations any more than man is a collection of wants. It takes a whole range of values mutually interpenetrating to constitute a community, or even a culture. We may note again, with approval, the comment by MacIver:[62] "Every society is held together by a myth-system, a complex of dominating thought-forms that determines and sustains all its activities. All social relations, the very texture of human society, are myth-born and myth-sustained." By myths MacIver means the "value-impregnated beliefs and notions that men hold, that they live by or live for." The realm of values has an autonomy of its own which must not be confused with the process of technology in the community.

In an actual small community we shall probably find the five characteristics which Brownell stresses in two of his studies:[63] "(1) A community is a group of neighbors who know one another face to face. (2) It is a diversified group as to age, sex, skill, function, and mutual service to each other. (3) It is a cooperative group in which many of the main activities are carried on together. (4) It is a group having a sense of 'belonging,' or group identity and solidarity. (5) It is a rather small group, such as the family, village, or small town, in which each person can know a number of others as whole persons, not as functional fragments." For the purposes of this essay we need not accent the geographical neighborhood, but it is significant to note that group life which is only associational may tear the community apart and may tend to reduce persons to mere role playing and to a congeries of "functional fragments." In a community common values are self-enforcing.

Since there is thus a fundamental difference between the principles of association and community, it is necessary to take a normative view of community as the matrix in which persons come to self-actualization. Associations even when they are wholeheartedly entered into by persons tend to function as levers, as pressures, and as power constellations in the community and in society at large. Associations are frequently related to the phenomenon of manipulation of persons for special ends and hence in opposition to personality as self-determinative. With the clarification of these two ideas we may bring this chapter to a close.

The essentially environmentalist approach to man is related to the tendency in associations to manipulate man. There is ample evidence that propaganda groups use their knowledge of psychological mechanisms to produce certain ideologies or emotional trends through rationally conceived methods. This manipulative attitude comes to the fore at the very time, says Mannheim, when the concern for personality in community is in a state of crisis.[64] We speak a great deal about community because this experience is becoming increasingly rare. We speak of person-to-person relations in a growing impersonal urban situation "with that flavor of ideological beatification, which in itself indicates a certain loss of reality." " 'Thou experience' on the level of romantic elevation, is a compensating move of the mind in mass society and develops in strict correlation with the growth of the manipulative approach."[65] Mannheim finds the ultimate of real paradox in this process when the processes of mass communication are used, for example, the radio, to induce the primary experiences (community feelings and person-to-person appeals and what we call the human touch) by those in charge of manipulating the mind in society.

Yet this artificial and unwholesome situation only heightens the fact, which is also a problem in values, that persons are not treated for what they really are—ends in themselves. Thus the community becomes a problem for personality. The true and real community can be defined only in terms of the true and real person. Human beings become persons only when they really become self-determining. As a person his conduct is not simply imitative or the result of suggestion, or the slavish product of custom and habit, or quasi-automatic and subservient, devoid of understanding, or of insight into personal purposes. The person is a center of initiating activity, capable of choosing, of critical appraisal, and of love. Certainly, one of the criteria of the person is his capacity for whole response to whole people. What is important is not that he is different or divergent from other people but that he is morally autonomous, the subject of his own consciousness, truly responsible. Thus we find that our conception of the person is communitarian. The individual is not the enemy of society. What is given is interpersonal reality. But this social whole composed of lesser social groups is not an abstract flux of mere process. It exhibits to a marked degree a genuine community where each person is deeply involved in other persons, but in which each remains an end-in-himself.

The idea of community is thus both a descriptive and a normative term. Community is a sociological and metaphysical fact, but it is also an axiological category underlying anthropology and the other social sciences, on the one hand, and ethics on the other. Social ethics must take into consideration all that is known clinically about person-in-community. But it must also develop appropriate communitarian norms in politics, economic relations, social welfare, international relations, and the like. Democracy, education, labor-management relations, programs of rehabilitation and reconstruction should be shaped accordingly. Democracy is not soundly grounded when it is based on individualism alone or viewed merely as a type of association. Government is not to be simply identified with community, but its authority is grounded in community. Likewise, education is not soundly grounded when it wavers between mere individual permissiveness, on the one hand, and authoritarianism, on the other. The communitarian ideal in education is not a midpoint between these, but a third type of group relationship in which the members learn to participate critically, creatively, and responsibly. So also in industrial relations the true path to social justice is found neither in individualism and limited interest associations, on the one hand, nor in collectivism which destroys individuality, on the other. The fact that human nature behaves at its best in small groups, all other things being equal, points to more humane group personnel relationships in the factory and in the union. Men are not solitaries, neither are they mere fuel for the conflicts of society. In all social policy the dignity of personhood must go hand-in-hand with realization in community responsibility.

Paradoxical as it may seem, social solidarity rightly conceived is markedly pluralistic. Interdependence, mutual aid, group discipline, and freedom belong in one concrete whole. Social ethics must therefore consider community as an organic pluralism. Personal freedom finds its highest expression in rational love, the person finding his fulfillment in productive labor and brotherly responsibility and the community planning its life not only in terms of social minimums and common necessities, but in terms of the safeguarding and enhancement of the freedom which is fully personal. What personalism offers as a social philosophy is the hypothesis that community conceived normatively as rational love and as organic pluralism is consistent and coherent with the metaphysical actualization of the person.

III

THE STRUCTURE AND PREDICAMENT
OF RESPONSIBILITY

Responsible action presents both a structure and a predicament. In the present and succeeding chapters the moral structure of responsibility will primarily engage our attention. The discussion will seek to illuminate the moral laws which compose the norms of this structure. These moral laws may also be called the universal principles to which in making choices the will ought to conform.[1] From the outset it must be noted that universal principles of this type do not prescribe the specific ethical standards, or codes, of any particular religion or society. They are methodological and regulative, but not constitutive of the cultural content of personal decision or social policy. They are structural and normative for all societies when applied in their interrelated wholeness.

Several problems will immediately arise in the mind of the reader, problems which relate to the predicament of responsible action, and to these we must give attention here, especially because postponement may create basic misunderstandings about this book as a whole and its underlying theory. The dynamics of man's predicament as a responsible actor are not the main concern of this discussion, but a recognition of the nature, function, and importance of this predicament will serve to give a proper setting for the problems especially selected for inquiry.

A. FACTORS IN A MORAL SITUATION

Moral situations are complex wholes. A person in a moral situation is confronted by a number of factors commonly recognized by students of ethical theory. A review will be illuminating.

From the standpoint of the actor a moral situation involves the following: (1) examining and clarifying the alternatives from which to choose; (2) elaborating rationally the consequences of the alternatives; (3) projecting the self imaginatively into the predicted situation, that is, making a dramatic identification of the present self with the future self in the envisaged situation; (4) identifying the self imaginatively with the points of view of those persons whom the proposed act will most seriously affect; (5) estimating and comparing the values involved in each of the projected consequential situations and comparing these situations; (6) deciding; and (7) acting.[2] In a moral situation so outlined we recognize factors such as value, ought, possible alternatives, inclinations, preferences, reason, moral insight, choice, standards, means, ends, selfhood, persons, and society. These must be understood in relation to each other and as a whole. They constitute significant concepts in ethics and illuminate its definition.

"Ethics," writes Maurice Mandelbaum, "is the attempt to gain a systematic and complete understanding of moral experience."[3] It is a normative discipline since it deals with standards. Edgar S. Brightman defines ethics "as *the normative science of morals,* which means that it is the attempt to discover and justify reasonable standards of conduct."[4] Lucius Garvin offers a similar definition: "Ethics is the critical study of standards for judging the rightness or wrongness of conduct."[5] This carries thought along to the more inclusive definition of ethics as *"the normative science of the principles (or laws) of the best types of human conduct."*[6] Principles must be found which deal with the total moral situation, more especially with values and ideals (norms) and obligation (ought or duty). Such principles are laws which make a demand on choice.

Moral experience comprises choice, norms, values, and obligation which are not wholly taken into account by the descriptive sciences such as psychology and sociology. Psychology and sociology make important contributions to ethics. Psychology can throw a great deal of light on the sources of moral judgments. It can help in clarifying the relationship between moral judgments and conduct. Conduct as here used means behavior involving choice, that is, behavior which is critically and selectively controlled. Sociology helps disclose the determinants as well as the content of many moral judgments. It can show which moral judgments are effective in a given society and why it is that in all societies we find moral judgments.[7] Both psychology and sociology throw a great deal of light on responsibility as response among persons and groups as they seek to achieve certain goals. A scientific description of response illuminates the phenomenon of responsibility, but such illumination must be distinguished from the normative laws of obligation and value. Psychology and sociology can help illuminate many facets of what we have called the human predicament. They should not, however, be confused with the theological or philosophical interpretation of man's ultimate situation. Contrariwise, the generalizations of theology must not be substituted in empirical analysis for the hypotheses of behavioral sciences.

Ethics, we have noted, deals with willed action. Here the source of action is the self; the actor is in the center of the action and feels responsibility for his actions. The moral nature of a man's action is thus a matter of choosing. To be morally aware is to be aware of choice or decision. Moral deliberation leading to decision and action involves choosing among alternatives. Here again Mandelbaum's phenomenological analysis seems to be correct: "It is . . . the fact that in some choices we feel that one of the alternatives places a *demand* upon us, that we are obliged, or bound, to act for it. This feeling of obligation appears as being independent of preference, as many of the alternatives within our experience do not. Where neither alternative has this character, where our choices are wholly matters of preference or desire, the choice which we face does not appear as a moral choice. However, let either alternative appear not as a preference but as an 'objective' demand, and I feel myself to be confronted by a moral issue, by a categorical imperative, by an injunctive force which issues from one of the alternatives itself."[8]

B. THE MORAL LAWS

What are the moral laws which we propose to offer as the systematic alternative to traditional natural law theories and which are latent in Christian ethics as described in Chapter I? They are a system of eleven laws developed by E. S. Brightman, three additional laws formulated by L. Harold DeWolf, and a metaphysical law.[9] After stating the laws we shall present a brief exposition of their nature. We shall then relate these laws to man's predicament viewed from a religious perspective. In the immediately succeeding chapters we shall more fully relate these laws to the general concept of responsibility.

The first group of laws is *formal*. They raise the question "How ought we to choose?" and answer "Consistently."

1. The Logical Law:

"All persons ought to will logically; i.e., each person ought to will to be free from self-contradiction and to be consistent in his intentions. A moral person does not both will and not will the same ends; this property of a moral person is called his formal rightness."[10]

2. The Law of Autonomy:

"All persons ought to recognize themselves as obligated to choose in accordance with the ideals which they acknowledge. Or: Self-imposed ideals are imperative."[11]

These two principles have to do with the will alone, stating norms to which a reasonable will must conform irrespective of the ends (values) which the will seeks to realize. Ethical studies which deal with these problems alone, though indispensable, are only partial treatments of the whole ethic of personality.

The second group of laws is *axiological*. This means that they state the principles which the ends (values) willed by the good will ought to embody. They raise the question "What should we choose?" and answer "Coherent values." These principles are the laws governing the choice of values.

3. The Axiological Law:

"All persons ought to choose values which are self-consistent, harmonious, and coherent, not values which are contradictory or incoherent with one another."[12]

4. The Law of Consequences:

"All persons ought to consider and, on the whole, approve the foreseeable consequences of each of their choices. Stated otherwise: Choose with a view to the long run, not merely to the present act."[13]

5. The Law of the Best Possible:

"All persons ought to will the best possible values in every situation; hence, if possible, to improve every situation."[14]

6. The Law of Specification:

"All persons ought, in any given situation, to develop the value or values specifically relevant to that situation."[15]

7. The Law of the Most Inclusive End:

"All persons ought to choose a coherent life in which the widest possible range of value is realized."[16]

8. The Law of Ideal Control:

"All persons ought to control their empirical values by ideal values."[17]

The third group of laws is *personalistic*. They analyze the moral laws of personality as a whole, indicating what ought to follow in conduct from the fact that value is always the experience of persons. These laws ask "For whose sake should we choose?" and answer "For self, for others, and for the ideal person."

9. The Law of Individualism:

"Each person ought to realize in his own experience the maximum value of which he is capable in harmony with moral law."[18]

10. The Law of Altruism:

"Each person ought to respect all other persons as ends in themselves, and, as far as possible, to co-operate with others in the production and enjoyment of shared values."[19]

11. The Law of the Ideal of Personality:

"All persons ought to judge and guide all of their acts by their ideal conception (in harmony with the other Laws) of what the whole personality ought to become both individually and socially."[20]

The fourth group of laws comprises the *communitarian* laws. They are the moral laws of community. They place the free and responsible person in the context of a free and responsible society. To the question "In what social context shall we choose?" they respond "For the whole community as requiring to be perfected."

12. The Law of Co-operation:

"All persons ought as far as possible to co-operate with other persons in the production and enjoyment of shared values."

13. The Law of Social Devotion:

"All persons ought to devote themselves to serving the best interests of the group and to subordinate personal gain to social gain."

14. The Law of the Ideal of Community:

"All persons ought to form and choose all of their ideals and values in loyalty to their ideals (in harmony with the other Laws) of what the whole community ought to become; and to participate responsibly in groups to help them similarly choose and form all their ideals and choices."

The reader will note certain traits of this system of moral laws. First of all they comprise a system because moral experience is a whole. They are derived by analyzing all the principal aspects of moral situations and the moral life and then formulating the universal principles which comprise a coherent unity. Mandelbaum observes that "all moral judgments are grounded in our apprehension of relations of fittingness or unfittingness between the responses of a human being and the demands which inhere in the situation by which he is faced."[21] This is like Brightman's principle of empirical coherence. No moral law can be fully grasped in isolation from the other moral laws, for each is logically abstracted from the whole. Thinkers of all ages have agreed to the spirit of the systematic structure of the moral order. Plato, Aristotle, Spinoza, Hegel, Schleiermacher, Bradley, Rashdall, Dewey, and many others have stressed the organic relatedness of basic ethical principles.

Another characteristic of this system of moral laws is its rationality. What are the nature and function of reason as here understood? Reason is a function of the self as it seeks to understand the various aspects of reality by being open to them impartially and permitting them to give their testimony, then developing hypotheses which will remove inconsistencies in the testimony, and finally organizing the parts into a coherent whole where possible. Reason is a function whereby the mind seeks to keep all facets of experience actively communicating with and controlled by the rest. As Peter Bertocci says, "Reason must allow every part to speak, but it must go on to assess the relation of the parts to each other with a view to discovering what the testimony of the whole reveals."[22] Reason cannot allow any part of experience special privilege or protection in the intercourse of ideas or as an arbitrary determiner of the meaning of experience as a whole. Reason opens the door to Christian experience and revelation but insists that they establish their claims by the same norms as judge all counterclaims.

A third quality of the moral laws is that they do not prescribe antecedently any special cultural content. They are methodological and regulative. They are normative principles of criticism. Such laws are sometimes dismissed as rational common sense and as having therefore no distinctive place in Christian social ethics. If the criticism that they are common sense were valid, it would only confirm their moral necessity. As a matter of fact Christian theologians often appeal to one or more of them to justify action without being fully aware of what they have done. If these are the principles to which Christian moralists appeal in judging or initiating conduct, their formulation and expression are important. Neglecting them as regulatory and methodological laws may mean that thinkers and moral agents assume that they are employing other principles when, in fact, these norms have been appealed to and applied. Barth, Lehmann, and Ramsey seem to do this.

An illustration from a discussion of race relations by Reinhold Niebuhr will clarify the basic issue here. The issue he seeks to handle is stated in the title of his essay "What Resources Can the Christian Church Offer to Meet the Crisis in Race Relations?"[23] His analysis makes the following points leading up to action based on prudential judgments. Niebuhr says, first of all, that it would be wrong to assume that there are automatic resources of grace and wisdom even in the church. In fact, on the race issue the church has not been very creative. The reason? "Perhaps it lacks resources for discriminate judgment—and that is the kind of judgment that the problem demands."

What are the resources for discriminate judgment? He does not state them but gives hints of their nature. These seem to point to the kinds of moral law with which this and later chapters are concerned. Niebuhr asks for sympathy for the Negro who has been smarting under age-old patterns and who is now, since the famous Supreme Court decision of 1954, in a new environment. He appeals to the dignity of man. He asks for awareness of the predicament of parents of school children who know that a wide cultural difference exists between the children of the two races. He also points forward to the day when these will be rectified. Finally he states that great prudence is required and observes that charity is the father of prudence. After appealing to prudence he says that it is not part of the Christian ethic. What the Christian ethic contributes is the insight that none of our judgments are pure and that even the best of them are corrupted by the perennial sin of group pride. Although the gospel makes a rigorous moral demand, it knows that all men fall short of universal love.

If there is to be action, there must be a discriminate judgment. Is the latter only an ethical intuition of a subjective sort—albeit of a person as perceptive as Reinhold Niebuhr? A further analysis reveals an impressive list of appeals to several of the moral laws. In his quest for a sound prudential judgment in race relations Niebuhr appeals to an ideal of *community* relations, to the value of *personality,* to the need to control the present crisis by moral

ideals, to the need to consider a wide range of *values,* to awareness of *consequences,* to concern not only for individual *self* but
others, to doing the *best possible* under the circumstances, and to
do that which is specifically *relevant* in the situation. Such action
will include a witness of *integrity* in the midst of compromise.
These criteria of prudential judgments are moral norms. Apart
from them the appeal to prudence and discriminate judgment is
but a plea either to a special situational revelation or intuition—
methods which Niebuhr repudiates. We must conclude, then, that
moral principles are required which supplement the special appeals to charity and humility which Niebuhr emphasizes in the
Christian ethic.

C. MORAL LAW AND THE PREDICAMENT OF MAN

The discussion of the structure of a moral situation and the
system of moral principles brings us, once more, to consider their
relation to the problems which concern theological ethics. In
terms of contemporary debate this means the relation of norms to
the predicament of man.

To speak of responsibility is to acknowledge that men are often
irresponsible. To stress norms means that men violate them. To
seek the good society means that men live in imperfect and unjust
societies. To command obedience to moral law means to acknowledge the facts of disobedience and immorality. In short, the
structure of responsibility points to a pervasive human predicament. Moral dilemmas raise the questions "Who is this man who
in the midst of evil seeks and wills the good?" and "Who is this
man who in the midst of ultimate good seeks and wills transient
evil?" The answers to these questions point to the realm of redemption and to man's ultimate destiny. Failure to acknowledge
both the dilemmas and the theological issues they raise is a major
source of conflict between much philosophical and theological
thought.

The predicament of man includes such facts as these: he is not
only a seeker of righteousness, but often self-righteous; he not
only honors humility in word, but is often proud and haughty; he not
only loves others, but is guilty of self-love; he not only seeks the

holy, but is sensual and secular; he not only aims at the highest good, but often he pretends to possess it; he not only expresses his freedom, but is anxious; he not only can know God, but he frequently fails to trust him; he not only loves the good, but he is mixed in his affections and motivations; he is not only capable of reason, but he rationalizes; he not only perceives his self-worth, but overvalues himself; he not only knows many good things, but he lacks the power to have them; he is not only a creature, but he mismanages and betrays his creatureliness.

His predicament comprises also the converse of these dilemmas.

Such a list of human dilemmas could be extended almost indefinitely. There is not only an inexhaustible range of values to be achieved; there seems to be an unlimited number of ways to fail or betray them.

No man's individual acts of loyalty and disloyalty, of goal seeking or goal rejection, are isolated from his whole response to the whole demand of reality upon him. His relations to his fellowmen are involved in and transcended by his relations to himself and to God, his ultimate ground and value. Consequently, his relation to moral law is always conditioned by his relation to God's action in and for him. Man's understanding of the ultimate relationships in which he stands to his God (whether as Creator, Redeemer, or Holy Spirit) affects qualitatively how he relates himself to the structure of moral responsibility.

The predicament of man includes not only moral dilemmas but also uncertainties, doubts, and fears. He cannot prove with rational certainty that God exists, that he revealed himself fully and uniquely in Jesus Christ, and that life endures with meaningful personal existence beyond the grave. On these matters man may have a religious faith buttressed by practical certitude through empirical coherence. Yet the predicaments of doubt and fear are present. And few respond with genuine trust and Christian thrust.

Fear of death plays a more powerful role in most critical life situations than most men realize. Man, who by the creative act of God first enters life through the door of birth, finds before him the inevitable door of death awaiting him at the end of his physical adventure no matter what journey he has undertaken from the one door to the other. Fear of death is the arch-fear of all particular fears and anxiety. Fear of death is the tap-root of all terror reactions. It enters continually into man's dramatic struggle with freedom and causality.

Faith and reason, theology and philosophy, may successfully cope with these predicaments but they cannot entirely eliminate them. They surround every moment of decision and action. For this reason the problem of ethics must be considered not only in terms of its own relative autonomy but in the context of religion.

Religion thus deals with those personal and social ideas, attitudes, and practices by means of which man struggles with the ultimate questions of life. Such questions, as we have seen, include the meaningfulness of life itself, the quest for fulfillment and its frustrations, the hostilities that are engendered in conflicts with oneself and others, the guilt that is engendered by alienation from God and one's neighbors, the fact of death, the ways in which good triumphs over evil or faith and love overcome anxiety and alienation. In Chapter IX we shall note the conception of Christ which provides an ultimate religious answer to the demand for a responsible person in a responsible society. He is both the cosmic ground of the responsive community and personal power in human history. Through him men may accept and achieve victory over their predicaments.

The predicament of man is manifested both by the ambiguity of many moral situations and by the inability of man to guarantee the conservation of moral value. He needs the sustaining strength of more-than-human power and God's acceptance of his effort and faltering trust in the midst of ambiguous moral choices. The Pauline assurance that man is "justified by faith" is an important Christian foundation. It defines a relationship that transcends though it does not set aside either moral law as defined in this book nor the imperative demand of a concrete duty once it has been apprehended.

Because man's basic predicaments are overcome only in and through God's own love of man, there is a tendency in some theology to take a pessimistic view of human nature, of society, and of history. Some writers are so impressed with sin and failure that they generalize as follows: individual social problems can be solved but not *the* social problem. Others state that man is so inwardly compromised and sinful that no real moral progress can ever be achieved. As good grows, evil does the more abound. This view is taken as more "realistic" than a doctrine of man that is more confident or optimistic. Those who seek with enthusiasm to solve some grave problem, as for example in race relations, are deterred by warnings about the dangers of self-righteousness and the universal guilt in man and groups. Pessimism tends in this way to cut the vital nerve of moral responsibility.

Another tendency in theology is to view moral situations as so complex that no rational principles are applicable to them. Social action is then criticized as always guilty of over-simplification. Here an ultimate perspective is used to repudiate all ambiguous efforts as presumptuous assertion of man's own ideals and idolatrous programs. Obsession with the complex produces confusion, despair, complacency, and even apathy.

Yet another way of handling man's predicament is to hold that love so greatly transcends moral law that one cannot appeal to principle in any concrete situation. The good in each situation is so unique and love transcends law so completely, the argument runs, that no Christian social policy is possible. Ethical judgments are essentially oracular prophetic utterances having no generally rational structure or universal relevance. Such an ethic separates the ultimate perspective and role of love so radically from justice that it is difficult to see how any responsible social policy would ever be possible on that basis.

As a corrective to sentimentality, easy optimism, and complacency, a "realistic" view of human nature and conduct makes a significant contribution. It must be frankly acknowledged that persons do not easily win a victory over sensuality, self-interest, self-centeredness, and selfishness. It must be fully recognized that many social groups are dominated by limited interests which have a disintegrating effect on community. The principle of community, as distinguished from that of associations with limited interests, does not automatically assure the redemptive release of love

sufficient to solve social questions. Other major emphases of the
"realistic" school may also be acknowledged with approval: that
lifting up an ideal does not assure repentance; that much contemporary preaching is sheer sentimentality; that all group life is
pervaded by varying degrees and kinds of coercion; that individual consciences are on the whole more sensitive to the highest
good and more willing to sacrifice for it than are most social
groups; and that there is no historical principle of guaranteed
progress.

But a corrective theology is not of itself an adequate doctrine
of personal and social redemption. For this task the empirical
coherence of faith and reason and the supplementary approach of
philosophical and theological ethics are essential. Ultimate beliefs
must be united with the rational principles that control discriminate judgments in concrete situations.

The quest for empirical coherence in Christian social ethics as
an interdisciplinary field of study indicates the need for a transi-
tional law standing between ethics on the one hand and metaphysics, philosophy of religion, and theology, on the other.

15. This law DeWolf has called *the metaphysical law:* "All
persons ought to seek to know the source and significance of the
harmony and universality of these laws, i.e., of the coherence of
the moral order." A full exposition of such coherence would take
us beyond the limits of this volume. Since our main interest is to
supply the defect in Christian ethics of providing for the type of
moral law herein developed, there are many issues in the relationship of theological and philosophical ethics—the methods and
assumptions of philosophy and theology—which have to be de-
ferred for consideration. Nevertheless the meaning and significance of Jesus Christ in relation to responsible personhood and
community must be dealt with, however briefly. While Christian
ethics is not prescriptive, it brings to Christian social ethics the
category of *agape* in the concrete personhood of Jesus Christ. He
does not change the structure of moral law but he transforms
value, virtue, and culture.

IV

MORAL LAWS: THE FORMAL ASPECTS

To make the transition from theological ultimates and philosophical ideal ends to concrete decisions requires an appeal to moral law. The moral laws to be defined and expounded in the next four chapters may be regarded as principles of discriminating choice. They are not "middle axioms" in the sense developed by John Bennett in *Christian Ethics and Social Policy* and as used in ecumenical discussions on church and society since the Oxford Conference of 1937. These moral laws ought all to be obeyed in formulating any middle axiom, but they do not appeal to a substantive moral consensus or to substantive common ground morality. These moral laws are useful in several dimensions but their validity is found in their rational and empirical coherence as they come to terms philosophically with the whole range of moral data. They are laws of choice. The task of defining middle axioms comes logically after the coherence of these moral laws with Christian ethical faith has been accomplished.

Moral law develops logically from the formal law to the metaphysical law. The ultimate source and ground of ethics ought to be considered. Moral law builds conceptual bridges from the idea of God to concrete situations without compromising the will of God or prejudging the situational outcome. Moral law is implied in common ground morality, but it offers principles of criticism for all moral consensus. It is thus vertical and horizontal in its applications. When used to design sound "middle axioms" it can probably replace the appeal to natural moral law. This part of our task we shall undertake when criticizing natural law.

As we have indicated earlier the moral laws are grouped into four levels, plus a final metaphysical law. These are the formal moral laws, the axiological laws, the laws of personality, and the communitarian laws.

The formal moral laws, the logical law, and the law of autonomy may appear so obvious that they are hardly worth mentioning. It would seem obvious to a well-tutored person that he should be consistent and that he should act in good faith. If a person says, "I ought to pay my bills," and at the same time says, "I ought not to pay my bills," the contradiction is so blatant as to rule out the possibility of his having any moral responsibility at all. If a person says, "I acknowledge that paying my bills is an ideal to which I ought to subscribe, but I do not propose to live by this ideal," he is not dealing with himself or his creditors in good faith. Clearly, if one does not choose in good faith one does not choose with consistency either. These illustrations deal with the specific value of paying one's bills but the principles, or laws, with which they are concerned in the present discussion refer to the formal aspects of choosing. The quality of the "ought" involved in each of these principles is so basic as to invite critical attention. Both Christian ethics and philosophical ethics must acknowledge these formal principles, or it is impossible, as will be shown, to discuss moral responsibility intelligently.

A. THE LOGICAL LAW

The logical law embodies the fundamental rational ideas of consistency and universality. Consistency refers to identity of meaning and universality refers to all possible instances of the class of objects intended. This appeal to consistency and universality is formally stated as follows: *"All persons ought to will logically; i.e., each person ought to will to be free from self-contradiction and to be consistent in his intentions. A moral person does not both will and not will the same ends; this property of a moral person is called his formal rightness."*[1] This law has to do only with the willing or intent, not with the act or the content of the will. Its function is not to give light on or to decide whether a given value claim is good or bad but to eliminate contradiction. The two ideas of consistency and universality to which the law appeals are logically implicit in all valid moral judgments, for a judgment regarding choice, a selective volition, has a cognitive component which is subject to elementary rational analysis. The logical "ought" involved in rational analysis is formally implied in the moral "ought" formulated in this law.

Mandelbaum has shown that a phenomenological analysis indicates the presence of the principles of consistency and universality in all moral judgments.[2] Several aspects or elements of moral judgments are noteworthy in this connection. Whenever a valid moral judgment is made, it asserts something which is not restricted by reference to the psychological or sociological conditions surrounding the judgment. That which is being morally judged is dominantly judged in terms of its cognitive structure. It does not suffice, therefore, to stress the influence of the so-called subjective states of emotion, sentiment, or personality which are projected into a moral situation. The reader can readily note that the appeal to universality and the factor of consistency (and contradiction) are present in the two judgments taken together that I ought to pay my bills and I ought not to pay my bills. Even in unique circumstances the moral assertion which is made implies or assumes that there is a universal involved in the judgment. "The principle of universality demands that we should not deny the assertoric character of moral judgments."[3] It should also be noted that the formal principle of intending consistency and universality is not static but is relevant to every stage of the dynamic process of moral experience.

Consistency and universality are closely related. The logical law of morals does not assert that persons should never change their minds. It does not deny that "new occasions teach new duties." But it does assert that in all changing circumstances a person ought to intend to be loyal to the formal principle underlying moral judgment. The primary proof of this and the other moral laws, as Brightman pointed out, is a dialectical one: "if you assume them to be false, impossible or irrational consequences will follow." Without universality and consistency no moral situation may be intelligently confronted. "The principle of universality states that, to be valid, a moral judgment must make an assertion which is not restricted by any reference to the time at which, conditions under which, or point of view from which it is made."[4]

The principle of consistency requires the faithful application of universality. Brightman and Mandelbaum do not reject the profound truth that underlies the much-quoted maxim: "A foolish consistency is the hobgoblin of little minds."[5] The problem, however, is in the term "foolish." New data may in fact obligate a change of view. "What is rejected as invalid is a drift or shift in point of view which is not accompanied by a denial of the truth of an assertion which was made from the previous point of view."[6] When Socrates laid great stress on consistent definition of moral concepts, he was employing the principle here involved. The principle of consistency does not prove the rightness or wrongness of a particular judgment, but it does make clear that there is a primacy in certain objective claims of fact and assertion.

The logical law is a principle of self-respect, for it is the principle of dogged self-criticism. It is the principle which earnestly espouses the quest for the mastery over self-deception. Richard Cabot[7] makes this focal in his whole approach to the meaning of ethics. Joseph Butler held that self-deception "is a corruption of the whole moral character in its principle."[8] The will to intend consistency does not guarantee non-deception, but it is the personal root of integrity in relation to both facts and values as they affect conduct.

One of the consequences of the refusal to acknowledge the logical moral law is the state of *anomie,*[9] or normlessness. For example I once knew a high school principal who held that for each situation one needed a different philosophy. His administration was full of tension and insecurity. Not being able to achieve coherence in his educational philosophy he surrendered consistency and fell into sheer irrationalism. Where there are no abiding norms, chaos reigns.[10] The logical law applies not only to ends but also to methods. *Anomie,* or the breakdown of standards in a society or culture, may arise not only because of inconsistent ends but also because the means to achieve them have been violated. To achieve certain goals like success, persons and groups often resort to breaking the rules of the game. When persons or groups do not will to choose and act in accordance with agreed upon rules the results spell social disintegration. This observation leads us directly to the other basic formal law, the law of autonomy.

B. THE LAW OF AUTONOMY

The moral life, on its formal side, is not only a matter of consistency but also of keeping faith. Richard Cabot has formulated this idea in terms of keeping one's agreements. He approaches the moral life by using three tools of moral insights, (1) the making of agreements, (2) the keeping of agreements, and (3) the revising or improving of agreements.[11] Such agreements are either with oneself or with others, either explicit or tacit. The law of autonomy underlies primarily (1) and (2). When one makes an agreement he makes it with himself to keep it in good faith with others. The idea of improving agreements with oneself and others carries the analysis of moral experience beyond the law under consideration. But even the improving of agreements is morally worthless, as well as futile, if there is no binding intention to keep the agreements. Moral insight presupposes moral autonomy and the irreducibility of "ought."

The law of autonomy says: *"All persons ought to recognize themselves as obligated to choose in accordance with the ideals which they acknowledge.* Or: *Self-imposed ideals are imperative."*[12] In the history of ethical theory the moral principle of autonomy is classically associated most closely with Immanuel Kant, and more particularly with his idea of the categorical imperative. He used the term "categorical imperative" to distinguish it sharply from hypothetical and prudential commands. So impressed was he by the basic significance of the principle that he affirmed it as the primary law of the good will. He said, "It is not possible to think of anything anywhere in the world, or even out of it, which could be regarded as good without limitation, with the single exception of a good will." The maxim of the categorical imperative is a positive demand, at once rational, volitional, unconditional, and universal: "Act only on that maxim which will enable you at the same time to will that it be a universal law."[13] This principle expresses a synthesis both of the logical law and the law of autonomy and affirms the primacy of the good will as a formal principle. Kant went so far as to make the autonomy of the will the sole principle of all moral laws. In affirming this he erred in making autonomy the sole principle, as will be shown later in this chapter. Nevertheless, the law of autonomy expresses the formal principle of conscience, of integrity, of sincerity, of personal responsibility, of duty, and of character.

This law has minimal content, but it is not therefore narrow or confined, for it states the fundamental moral principle of autonomy in the response of the person to values, norms, and ideals. In personal goodness there is an elementary component of pure response in motive, a sensitivity and binding acknowledgment to the needs, interests, and feelings of others. The will binds itself to that which it acknowledges as a worthy ideal. The will's fundamental relation to its acknowledged ideals is through a bond which is not a prudential ought but an intrinsic demand. Here at the center of the moral life is a dispositional quality of choosing—a decision to be guided by the objective demands which are worthy to be chosen. This decision is free in the sense that it is not a mere function of conditioning factors in the environment. It involves the self-transcendence of the actor within the moral situation so that the acknowledging of ideals may become determinative. No one else can make the moral decision for the self. The idea of obligation involves freedom of choice.

C. CRITICAL PROBLEMS INVOLVING THE FORMAL MORAL ASPECTS

The discussion of four kinds of problems will illuminate the basic contributions of the formal moral laws. These problems grow out of the discussions of Kant's categorical imperative among ethical theorists, the relation of autonomy to certain types of character, the alleged conflict between rational autonomy and the ethical principle of paradox, and the supposed opposition between the idea of autonomy and the theological affirmation of theonomy.

1. Limitations of Kant's Categorical Imperative

Kant's basic maxim is called the categorical imperative because it is a self-acknowledged unconditional command. Although the principle of autonomy is fundamental, it is incomplete and inadequate when taken alone. The need to press beyond it has characterized much ethical theory in the years since Kant first formulated it. In the first place, the emphasis on rational will is too rigorous when it sets reason and impulse too sharply in contrast to each other. Second, Kant made too absolute a distinction between the intrinsic quality of the will and the effects or consequence of acts of will. Third, the functions of reason and impulse are treated as if they were each "pre-ordained for a distinct purpose."[14] Consequently the motive of ethics for him is exclusively duty. Kant had too mechanistic and hedonistic a view of desire and hence fragmented natural desire and duty in the person. This psychological standpoint cannot be phenomenologically defended.

There are additional difficulties. Kant's application of universality can be used by persons who have values contradictory to his values. He was not fully aware of the role of values other than "formal oughtness" which motivated his argument. Then too, he did not provide for the resolution of the conflict of duties. In terms of Cabot's approach, Kant did not provide for the making of new and better (including more relevant) agreements. Another way of stating these latter difficulties is that Kant had an inadequate axiology, or theory of values. The logical law of contradiction (consistency and universality) appealed to in the formal moral laws can determine neither virtue nor the content of duty. Additional principles must be observed in the life of responsible value choice. Nevertheless, what is of lasting worth in Kant's formalism is the principle of autonomy, and what is of abiding significance in his value theory is the categorical imperative reformulated in terms of respect for selfhood: "So act as to treat humanity, whether in your own person or in that of any other, in every case as an end and never as merely a means."

The strengths and weakness of the Kantian approach to ethics appear in an analysis of conscience. Conscience has a formal aspect and a material aspect. Conscience develops. The nature of a mature conscience can be understood only at the conclusion of a full treatment of moral experience. Persons should act in good faith, but they should also develop an adequate faith. Self-imposed ideals are imperative, but the ideals should be worth self-imposition. Persons ought to be not only formally right; they ought to strive to be materially right.

The word "conscience" refers to a complex phenomenon with such component elements as the memory of past experiences with their overtones of pleasantness and unpleasantness; group judgments or the voice of the community in the self; the ideal society for which the person aspires, or other drives for integration and achievement; and the sense of moral obligation accompanying moral judgments. Other analytical elements could be added in a longer treatment. But in any case conscience has both social and individual components. Person and community interpenetrate in varying patterns of cultural development. Persons develop the kinds of consciences, by and large, which are appropriate to a total cultural configuration. Conscience begins uncritically, and character tends to be formed before persons have fully developed critical consciences. This is the reason that the critical conscience becomes prominent only in a culture that makes it a conscientious matter of education.

The voice of the critical conscience is possible only because the persons may develop a response to the law of autonomy and proceed to criticism of values. But the uncritical conscience, what Bergson called the source of obligation in the closed society, is not a command of the law of autonomy.

If a person is to grow morally his uncriticized good behavior is of itself no substitute for criticized though outwardly less acceptable behavior. Inherited, emotional, or uncritical conscience must be criticized.[15] "Prove all things, hold to that which is good," applies to the growing conscience. One major goal of maturity is the enlightened conscience. Along the whole pathway of enlightenment the maxim that "self-imposed ideals are imperative" obtains. At each stage of growth a person must acknowledge more adequate ideals and standards. As Edgar Brightman formulates the relationship he says: "Moral responsibility, as a corollary of the Law of Autonomy, means that man is responsible to himself. The ideals which he recognizes and imposes on himself are ideals which he has no excuse for not obeying. If, however, he does disobey them, reason requires that he give an account to himself of what he has done, judge his conduct by his ideals, hold himself responsible. Such responsibility is moral maturity; until it has been achieved one may be said to be morally still an infant."[16]

2. Character Types and Autonomy

The principle of autonomy in the formation of mature character finds contemporary support in the popular work *The Lonely Crowd*.[17] This book describes changing character types in American culture. Two of the types have special relevance for the present discussion. The authors call them the "inner-directed" and the "other-directed." Both of them fall short of the truly free or autonomous person.

The source of direction for the inner-directed individual is "inner" in the sense "that it is implanted early in life by the elders and directed toward generalized but nonetheless inescapably destined goals." A psychological mechanism figuratively called the gyroscope comes into operation. "This instrument, once it is set by the parents and other authorities, keeps the inner-directed person . . . 'on course' even when tradition, as responded to by his character, no longer dictates his moves. The inner-directed person becomes capable of maintaining a delicate balance between the demands upon him of his life goal and the buffetings of his external environment."[18]

The other-directed individual has his source in his contemporaries, his peer-groups. These contemporaries are either directly known or those with whom he is indirectly acquainted through friends and mass media. "This source is of course 'internalized' in the sense that dependence on it for guidance is implanted early. The goals toward which the other-directed person strives shift with that guidance: it is only the process of striving itself and the process of paying close attention to the signals from others that remain unaltered throughout life."[19]

In contrast to these two types (both of them essentially uncritical), Riesman and his associates place the autonomous person. The autonomous are those "who on the whole are capable of conforming to the behavioral norms of their society, but are free to choose whether to conform or not."[20] Other-directed persons are clearly immature since they have no real source of moral initiative. But even the inner-directed persons are in most cases driven to their goals by a behavioral gyroscope over whose speed and direction they have little control and of whose existence they may be hardly aware. They correspond to Brightman's type of uncritical conscience. The autonomous type of person, however, is capable of choosing goals and modulating his pace. "The goals, and the drive toward them, are rational, nonauthoritarian and noncompulsive for the autonomous"; for the other two types the goals are merely given. Autonomous persons accept social and political authority conditionally. They can co-operate with others in action while maintaining the right of private judgment. Autonomy is never an all-or-nothing affair. Autonomy demands heightened self-consciousness and the achievement of effective self-transcendence and powers of abstraction during active co-operation or interaction with others.[21] In the autonomous type of character the law of autonomy has grown into free effectiveness. Its validity as a norm stands unimpaired by the presence of immature inner-directed and *anomic* other-directed persons in society.

3. *Autonomy and Paradox*

The third group of issues have to do with the alleged opposition of autonomous reason to and consequent need for paradox in theological discussions of ethics. The term "paradox" has three principal usages. (1) It may refer to a proposition which is contrary to received opinion or expectation. In this connection there is often the implication that it is marvelous or incredible. (2) It may refer to a statement or proposition which on the face of it seems self-contradictory, absurd, or at variance with common sense, though on investigation it may prove to be well-founded. (3) It may be applied to a proposition or statement that is actually self-contradictory, or contrary to reason or ascertained truth, and so essentially absurd and false. In one or more of these usages the word "paradox" is interchanged with the term "dialectical" to the confusion of intelligible discourse. The impression is left that theology deals with a dialectically irrational and paradoxical life of faith in opposition to the man-made claims of reason. The law of autonomy would therefore seem to be in direct conflict with theological ethics.

In considering the alleged opposition of rational autonomy and paradox, it must be reaffirmed that formal logic and dialectic are not mutually exclusive disciplines.[22] Dialectical thinking, rightly understood, does not contradict the rational structure of thinking. It carries the process of affirmation and negation through a movement of thought which becomes progressively more synoptic and coherent. Hegel used this principle in a classical way. Brightman would agree with Tillich that dialectical thinking "transforms the static ontology behind the logical system of Aristotle and his followers into a dynamic ontology, largely under the influence of voluntaristic and historic motives rooted in the Christian interpretation of existence."[23] Brightman believes that the process of dialectical synopsis leads to a personalistic metaphysics. Tillich rejects personality as an ultimate principle in favor of the general idea of Being. But both insist that dialectical thinking which is anti-rational is simply poor thinking. Theology is as dependent as is any other discipline on logic to make sense out of its assertions. DeWolf has pointed out that if the obligation of consistency is denied, then nothing is implied by love or the ideal of love. Every hateful act can then be described as in a "paradoxical" and theologically desirable relation to Christian love.[24]

The notion, therefore, that theological ethics can be paradoxical in the sense of the third definition of paradox (contrary to reason) must be rejected. There is nothing inherently irrational in the idea that a statement is paradoxical in being opposed to the received opinion or expectation. Similarly Christian judgments may be said to be paradoxical in the sense of the second definition. Thus they are not inherently paradoxical, but paradoxical language or arguments may be used to express the many-sidedness and the polarities in Christian insights. Among contemporary Christian ethicists Reinhold Niebuhr has used "paradox" as a kind of tactic in argumentation.[25] Niebuhr seems to have feared the rational formulation of the Christian message.[26] But, as Tillich has correctly shown, Niebuhr is closer to rational dialectic than he realizes.[27] The literary use of paradox must not be confused with assertion of ultimate unreason.

4. *Autonomy and Theonomy*

A final group of issues relates to the claim that the principle of autonomy idolizes reason and therefore contradicts the principle of theonomy. The principle of autonomy is opposed not to theonomy (the ultimacy of God's government) but to heteronomy (law given to the will by some external power). Even in the latter relationship the situation is complex. External commands abound everywhere in society, including the church. External commands violate the principle of autonomy only when they are adopted as rules of moral action without regard to this principle. Persons are often compelled to do things against their wills. They do not on that account violate the principle. But if the will consents to a heteronomous suggestion from any source, such as desire, inclination, or society, which is contrary to the ideals which have been acknowledged (and without reconsideration of the merits of the ideals), the law of autonomy has suffered violation. It must not be inferred that heteronomous principles must necessarily be inconsistent in content with autonomous ideals. Heteronomous commands may have consistent and benevolent content, but as the language of politics says, good government is no substitute for self-government. Persons may make the ideals presented to them their own. "A self-imposed ideal need not be a self-manufactured one."[28] God is the ultimate source of ideal values or norms. No ideal or belief is morally binding until it has been acknowledged and self-imposed.

A proper appreciation of the principle of autonomy saves Christian ethics from being a "tail on a theological kite." The effort to base morality solely on the divine will as an independent, objective, and authoritative foundation was shown by Schopenhauer to be circular argument and by von Hartmann as lacking in moral insight. There is no way of ascribing anything to God at all without some appeal to human experience and insight. Not to recognize these factors critically makes of faith the puppet of arbitrary assertion. Hence an exclusively heteronomous law is not a truly moral law. True morality cannot be based on the will of another. Each man must stand on his own feet if he is to be a moral subject. God's will is morally binding on man when it is responded to and accepted to be right. God does not internally or externally coerce man's will. From God's side the relation is one of freedom and an invitation to respond in faith. All appeals to the righteousness of God presuppose the capacity of the human being to have moral insight into God's rightness. The principle of autonomy does not mean that ethics is self-centered. Not at all! But it protects the integrity of personality as man grows in spiritual insight.

Critically mature persons may have an awareness of moral distinctions quite independently of their adoption of religious faith.[29] The objectivity of their truth is not dependent on support extraneous to themselves. This does not prevent them from leading ultimately to religious truth and in this sense depending on it. This dependence, as H. D. Lewis has shown, is not of such a kind as to change the intrinsic character of moral obligation when it has been ascertained.[30]

There are two kinds of obligation or duty, the one subjective and the other objective. The former refers to a man's being loyal to his own moral end or ideal. The latter is the course of action which he would consider his duty if he understood aright. It is the kind of duty we have in mind when we say that an honest or well-meaning person has done what is wrong.[31] The conscience of such a person who has done his objective duty is informed by and coherent with the whole of moral law. This objective kind of duty cannot be grasped under the law of autonomy taken alone, but requires the axiological, personalistic, and communitarian laws.

If we believe that God requires objective duty, then it is consistent to believe that God also requires subjective loyalty to obligation. Indeed, an adequate theology would seem to affirm that God wills men to develop precisely the freedom of self-imposition of acknowledged ideals in order to become what the Bible calls sons of God. On the other hand the ideal which is self-imposed may fall short of the good which God may objectively will for man. This will of God for man (as content of good or

right) is the object of man's quest. Man does not readily know
what this is in concrete situations. Man always knows his duty,
however, in the sense that moral obligation is directly related to
the intention to be loyal to self-imposed ideals. This sincerity
must never be compromised. "I ought, therefore I can." Only confusion results when objective duty is allowed to obliterate the
moral primacy of subjective duty. But only abstract or formal
goodness results when autonomy is not integrated with the axiological laws, the moral laws of value.

V

MORAL LAWS: THE AXIOLOGICAL ASPECTS

Values pervade moral experience. The moral principles which deal with values are called axiological laws. They presuppose the formal moral laws. The term "axiology" came into general usage in the nineteenth century to cover the whole theory of value, including psychological, sociological, anthropological, logical, ethical, aesthetic, religious, and metaphysical aspects of value. In this broad sense it includes both descriptive and normative theories. As used by Brightman in developing the axiological laws in ethics, axiology includes the theory of true value, or the theory of "ought" in the broadest sense. The moral laws thus point to an ultimate metaphysical perspective as well as to that of the actor in experiencing, choosing, and criticizing value.

A. THE REALM OF VALUES

The transition from the formal moral laws to the axiological laws carries thought into the realm of values. This vast domain of experience is world-wide and cosmic. It has both subjective and objective aspects. As used in this discussion the term "value" in its most elementary sense will mean "whatever is liked, prized, esteemed, desired, approved or enjoyed by anyone at anytime. It is the actual experience of enjoying a desired object or activity. Hence, value is an existing realization of desire."[1] In this definition there is recognition both of present experience and objective reference.

The problem of moral judgment does not arise until a norm of values is employed. Simply to say that I value some thing is not ethics. But when I admire some thing or event or action I mean that it is a "fitting object of admiration."[2] The quality of being admirable and the act of admiring are correlatives because there is

a normative judgment involved. Moral laws take account of value
description; but they relate the values described to norms, and
hence are normative.

Men desire many things. They are goal-seeking beings. Goal-
seeking activity is also called conative, or purposive, or teleological. Another description for such processes is that persons seek to
satisfy wants or needs; they relate means to ends. These activities
or processes raise questions as to whether there are common or
basic needs to be found in all cultures; whether values are intrinsic; and how values relate to each other. Are there cross-
cultural norms? There seem to be grounds for asserting many
more common values and norms in different cultures than is
usually supposed.[3] On a practical level persons often seek a consensus of values drawn from widely different cultural sources.

Today people are impressed by the pervasiveness of the value
of science in all parts of the world, though some do not admire or
appreciate it. But other values like courage, loyalty, and co-
operation may be as generally prized as is science. What types of
experience should be valued as normative? Is science universally
valid? Anthropologists sometimes give the impression that all cultural values are relative. We must then ask relative to what? The
scientific work of the anthropologists assumes the power of scientific method to arrive at truth. Here then are an ideal and a method
which may not be treated as cultural oddities or as meaningful
only in terms of the culture of the anthropologist. Anthropological
method has shown the existence of transcultural themes or values.

Science is sometimes regarded as neutral with respect to values.
The spread of scientific attitudes and methods, however, does
not lessen the problem of values but only adds to its complexity
and urgency. We can, therefore, see that a study of values carries
us into a vast domain of the interpenetration of values and norms,
means and ends. We cannot ignore the *truth* of modern science.
Once discovered, the truths of modern science and technology are
a universal possession of humanity, for they are not only human
truths, but accord in some degree with cosmic reality.

The axiological laws deal with the rational principles by which
values ought to be chosen. They command an intelligent choice of

values and of ordering among values. They command a more objective and teleological point of view as well as more observation of empirical details in values than do the formal laws. Hence it is easier to *know* when one is faithful to the formal laws than to the axiological laws.

The moral agent must consider whether the values to be chosen are self-consistent, harmonious, or coherent. The general axiological law raises these questions in addition: how do values relate to norms; how do intrinsic and instrumental values interpenetrate; and are values organized in a hierarchy? When the acting self confronts alternatives, he must consider consequences. The law of consequences raises the question of causal relationships among facts and values. After alternatives have been responsibly elaborated, the actor must will the best possible value in his situation. This moral law is often appealed to by those who try to disavow it in the interest of absolute values. Not only must a person choose in the light of the best possible, but he must choose the value or values specifically relevant to his situation. Consequently the law of specification points to the plurality of concrete duties in man's changing roles in society. The dangers of pluralism are corrected by the law of the most inclusive end which demands a life plan. This law brings harmony out of diversity. But a life plan must stand under the norm of ideals and be guided by it. Not only do consequences need evaluations but ideals also need criticism. Here the vision of perfection calls for the fulfillment of the good life in ever increasing measure. We must now consider these laws in greater detail showing how they evaluate critically the content of interest, preference, and desire and how they coherently provide the basis for an adequate life plan.

B. THE AXIOLOGICAL LAW

The general axiological law is as follows: *"All persons ought to choose values which are self-consistent, harmonious, and coherent, not values which are contradictory or incoherent with one another."*[4] The problem of values in the moral life is to find what is truly valuable in specific situations and in life as a whole. The law gives a general answer to the question "What is the *summum bonum,* or the greatest good?" In the New Testament the question is "What is the pearl of great price, or what will a man give in exchange for his life?"

No one can avoid choosing or evaluating experiences and events. If a chosen value is self-contradictory, it is impossible to realize it. When values interpenetrate, their realization involves them mutually. Therefore, if a value is incoherent with other chosen values, it involves contradictory choices and hence has violated the *logical law* presented in the previous chapter. When one chooses two contradictory values, at least one of these will violate an acknowledged ideal, and hence the *law of autonomy* will have been violated. The deliberate or careless choice of contradictory, inharmonious, or incompatible values violates the principle of integrity or sincerity and hence repudiates the very concept of character. Thus the laws so far considered have an intrinsic involvement in a moral whole. To the principle of consistency the moral laws of value add the principle of coherence. Paul Natorp has expressed the spirit of the general moral laws of value when he says, "The criterion of the ethical is found in the complete, law-abiding self-consistency of the ends of the individual subject and also of all subjects capable of will, thought of as united in a realm of ends."[5] Yet this law is close to the principle of autonomy in affirming a general moral imperative rather than any specific value experience. It commands no particular code or system of prescriptions. It does not begin a priori by choosing one culture in preference to another or one religion or ideology in favor of another. It begins with a broad empirical base and lifts up the norms of self-consistency, harmony, and coherence as principles of selection and organization. With Socrates it affirms that the unexamined life is not worth living, and with Hegel it affirms that the true is the whole.

To choose in accord with rational demands of consistency, harmony, and coherence requires not only a consideration of empirical values but also of ideal norms or types of values. Norms also must be self-consistent, harmonious, and coherent. Empirical values are the actual "spot values," the concrete datable experiences like going to the movies, eating a meal, visiting a friend, painting a picture, or running for political office. Ideals refer to the norms or conceptualized values of rational reflection and rational choice like honesty, sportsmanship, justice, freedom, equality, national loyalty, family preference, self-reliance, and self-sacrifice.

We shall note later how world community is related to commonly shared values and norms. What holds society together? The cohesive power of culture is sometimes called its myth-structure. In this sense myth means the value-impregnated beliefs which give unity and coherence to group life. We shall be led to ask whether there are common *themes* in man's variety of cultures which give promise of possible world unity or community. What, concretely speaking, are these *thematic* values? How are these *thematic values* related to basic human needs, and how, for example, are they related to the great effort of the Commission on Human Rights of the United Nations to formulate and seek adoption of a body of universal rights and freedoms? Do the alleged rights and freedoms of the Declaration of Human Rights adopted in 1948 by the General Assembly conform to the requirements of the axiological law?

This axiological law of itself leaves many problems unresolved. Among these are: (1) how ideal values are derived from empirical values; (2) whether ideals or norms are "revealed," "intuited," arbitrarily posited by persons, or have some other source; (3) whether any values are intrinsic, whether all values are instrumental, and whether intrinsic and instrumental values interpenetrate; and (4) whether the intelligently chosen life of value comprises values chosen in harmony with a hierarchy of values. If there is no strict hierarchy of ideals, is there a realm of coherent values organized according to some other principle? These questions will be illuminated as we consider the whole system of moral laws.

What is a true norm? In a provisional way we may state that those ideals which form a coherent system among themselves and have roots and fruits in a coherent organization and ongoing of actual value experience are true norms. The criticism, systematization, and development of spot-values (value claims, empirical values) by means of norms lead the moral actor from empirical values to true values. This position is essentially that taken by Brightman, who argued that the criterion of value, as of fact, is empirical coherence, which forbids any static science or philosophy and commands inquiry into possibility of growth.[6]

This perspective is also occasionally approached in the Christian ethics of Reinhold Niebuhr. He says, "I have agreed with Kant in finding logic a provisional instrument of morals insofar as the logical principle in reason may prompt the self to consider its ends in terms of their relationship with a total and coherent system of ends."[7]

The claims of coherence among values raises the question, as we have seen, of intrinsic and instrumental values and their relation to hierarchy and empirical coherence. Intrinsic values do not depend upon any other values, while instrumental or extrinsic values are those which are valuable only because they lead to some intrinsic value. The intrinsic good, in the words of Aristotle, is sought "for its own sake and for the sake of which we wish everything else." Now, as Garvin[8] and others have pointed out, the relationships between means and ends may be very complex and shifting:

(1) The same values may serve as both means and end and may now function as relatively good and again as relatively bad.

(2) A value that is intrinsically good may be instrumentally bad. Loyalty to family may lead to disloyalty to the community.

(3) What is intrinsically bad may serve good ends, as in the case of some pain.

(4) The ends and aims which control our activities and which determine our direction of value selection are not all on the same plane. This raises the question of the hierarchy of ends. Is there a hierarchy of values despite the varying functions which they may have in differing situations and circumstances?

One well-known modern table of values is that proposed by W. G. Everett,[9] which lists them as follows: (1) Economic Values; (2) Bodily Values; (3) Values of Recreation; (4) Associational Values; (5) Character Values; (6) Aesthetic Values; (7) Intellectual Values; and (8) Religious Values.

Another interesting table is the one presented by Lucius Garvin:[10]

Types of Interest or Activity	Values Developed
Intellectual, Aesthetic, Religious	Knowledge, Beauty, Devotion
Social, Moral	Love, Friendship, Fellowship, Character
Work, Craftmanship	Joy of Creativity, Sense of Accomplishment
Recreational, Play	Relaxation, Fun
Economic	Wealth, Security, Worldly Success
Bodily, Physical	Sense-Satisfaction, Health

Reflection on these types of values makes it quite clear how difficult it is to arrange them into a strict standard order of ascendancy. Economic values would seem to be almost exclusively instrumental, but economic life involves many of the others. The Commission on the Church and Economic Life of the National Council of Churches published a symposium volume entitled *Goals of Economic Life* in which the perspectives of various disciplines and sciences show clearly how many values interpenetrate in economic life.[11] The formulation of an intelligent view of economic life rests upon informed decisions as to the *ends* which one desires as well as upon well-grounded knowledge as to the *means* by which they might be attained. Ends and means, values and technics, interact with one another at every point in economic life, as they do in all of life. The classic studies of sociology of religion by Max Weber, Ernst Troeltsch, and R. H. Tawney as well as more recent ones by K. Boulding and Canon Demant show how the virtues and spirit of religious living interpenetrate with those of economic activity.[12]

What is truly observed here of economic values is even more clearly true of all the others. Values interpenetrate and accordingly the distinction of means and ends is often overlooked. Thus Brightman points out that an object of interest, insofar as it is external to consciousness, is neither an intrinsic value nor any part of one. The object has a purely instrumental value. A painting may be an object of interest, but only the personal, conscious enjoyment of the painting is intrinsically valuable. The painting as external object is itself potential value, that is to say, instrumental. But even when this point is granted we have the problem as to whether any fixed place in a hierarchy of values can be assigned to the art of painting. Paintings are enjoyed in connection with worship, as are musical productions. But both may be enjoyed without any association with specifically religious activities. Religion has a high value because it has as its ultimate end the worship of God. Yet an intelligent religious experience is to be preferred to an irrational or merely sentimental worship. No single value can stand alone for the simple reason that all are aspects or expressions of more inclusive personal experiences. All values are of, by, and for persons. Values seem to form a system, within which coherence must be found or achieved, rather than ordered according to some a priori scale. Yet priorities must be found within the rich whole of value.

The quest for ordering a hierarchy of values is ancient. Plato and Aristotle placed a high value on the theoretical or contemplative experiences. Plotinus profoundly influenced Augustine and the Christian mystics in the same direction. Aquinas superimposed the theological hierarchy of faith, hope, and charity on the redefined virtues[13] of Aristotle's ethics. The ethical tradition from Aristotle to Aquinas is fundamentally oriented in teleology. All things tend toward their proper end. The highest good is God. There is a natural-supernatural order, according to Aquinas, which gives a hierarchical structure to all things temporal and spiritual. This is the key to understanding the whole social ethics of traditional Roman Catholic Christianity. Authority is assigned in accordance with the status and dignity of the function or end served by each institution and office as in family, school, society, state, and church. The question of the supreme end is asked also in the Presbyterian catechism: "What is the chief end of man?" The response is "Man's chief end is to glorify God, and to enjoy him forever."

The tension between an interpenetrating system of intrinsic and instrumental values and the efforts to establish fixed hierarchies of value and to institutionalize these will engage our discussion more fully below. These issues anticipate the functions of other moral laws. The next step that should be taken is to consider the law of consequences.

C. THE LAW OF CONSEQUENCES

"All persons ought to consider and, on the whole, approve the foreseeable consequences of each of their choices. Stated otherwise: *Choose with a view to the long run, not merely to the present act."*[14] When the acting self confronts alternatives among which he must choose, he is obliged to consider the outcomes of these alternatives insofar as this is practically possible. The factor of consequences enters into the evaluation of competing claims. The law of consequences recognizes the truth in pragmatism that an exploration of the consequences of putting an idea into operation clarifies the meaning of the idea. This law is thus a principle of intelligence. It recognizes the forward reference of experience. It recognizes further that moral choices take place in a causal nexus and that the relations of means and ends are dynamic. Moreover, attending to consequences means noting their effects on the personality of the actor as well as on other persons and events. These effects need considering both in the short run and in the long run. Groups as well as individuals are generally more correct in assessing the short-run consequences of policies they espouse than they are of the long-run effects of their programs. Many practical idealists throw themselves into causes without responsibly calculating consequences and therefore often do more harm than good.

The law of consequences, we have said, is an appeal to intelligence. Brightman writes: "In proportion as we are intelligent, and desire to know what we are doing, we shall extend our knowledge of the effects of our choice from those now actually foreseen to all those which we can foresee with improved methods of investigation. Without such foresight we cannot tell what effect our act will have on the future conformity of our experience to moral law. . . . to will a cause the foreseeable effects of which one does not on the whole rationally approve (that is, approve as

in harmony with moral law) is to violate both the Law of Autonomy and the Axiological Law."[15] Concern for consequences
includes a concern for scientific and philosophic study of the
factual elements in value choices. It includes a program of serious
inquiry into the long-range as well as the short-range effects of
one's choices. Scientific knowledge makes responsible participation in social existence more fully possible.

The implementation of the law of consequences involves imaginative placement of the self in future situations both personal
and social. This requires the cultivation also of an imaginative
empathy with the experience of other persons in new contexts. To
be sure, not every moral situation is equally fecund with numer-
ous or significant consequences. Consequences involve questions
of more-or-less. Yet, it is an obligation to see if there are consequences and to consider those that are foreseeable.

In addition to its causal context a moral situation also has components of personal self-transcendence, freedom of alternative
choice, possibility, and evaluation. The moral law, then, which
specifically commands scientific awareness presupposes an actor
who is in command of the intelligent inquiry and who is free to
consider and approve alternative possibilities. Moreover, the
causal context has a depth dimension which is both personally
individual and socially horizontal. The situation is both cultural
and historical. Margaret Mead in *Cultural Patterns and Technical
Change* pleads for a comprehensive sensitivity on the part of
initiators of social change to the effects of technical change on
persons and groups in the areas involved.[16]

The appeal to consequences is one of the essential elements in
a teleological ethic and in what Max Weber called the ethics of
responsibility in contrast to the ethics of ultimate ends. Means
and ends form a complex unity. And the means we use tend to
determine the ends we get. Therefore, the end justifies the means
only if the whole situation has coherence and unity. It is very
difficult in complex matters, such as affect an economic order or
the state or a whole region, to apply the law of consequences.
But, since consequences are an objective aspect of policy-making,
an effort must be made to determine foreseeable effects.

Democratic nations appeal to the coherence of means and ends when they criticize the methods of totalitarian governments. Decent things, they say, must be decently done. One of the worst defects of communist regimes is their view that for an allegedly good end (a new classless society) any means is allowable (brainwashing, repression of political opposition, party purges, liquidations of large segments of the population, violence, etc.). Anticommunists in democratic countries often resort to means which tend to destroy democratic goals (attacks on civil liberties, violation of due process of law, restrictions on academic freedom, intimidation of the press). In the case of war as an instrument of national policy the question of the unity of means and ends reaches the heights of perplexity and moral ambiguity. How can a state, it is said, act responsibly if it is not willing to defend itself by war should that be necessary? On the other hand, since it is impossible to calculate the consequences of modern war and since the weapons now available threaten the very existence of life, the question must be pressed whether for an allegedly good end (group self-preservation) anything (total destruction) may be risked. In such a situation where the means used determine the end result, what is ultimately the moral difference between the policies of "democratic" and "totalitarian" nations?

The law of consequences leaves many ethical issues undecided: By what standard shall the approval of consequences be secured? How shall one deal with the never-completed task of describing probable consequences? How does one deal with situations which in principle seem to defy demonstration in terms of consequences? Moral controversy may arise from the different perspectives in which a range of consequences is regarded. There may be differences regarding the validity of the fundamental categories of explanation and evaluation with which two or more persons, groups, or societies approach a complex situation. There may be differences in the function assigned to remote as related to present circumstances in the light of an appeal to intrinsic rightness or wrongness.[17] The attempt to come to terms with these issues drives thought forward to the consideration of other axiological laws. In passing we may note the proposal by Mandelbaum that the apprehended goodness of certain consequences gives rise to a feeling of obligation to promote them only under certain conditions: (1) the goodness must appear as independent of our own inclinations or desires; (2) this goodness must attach to some envisioned future state of affairs which we feel we can help to actualize through action; (3) this state of affairs must be seen as relevant to our situation.[18] Moral laws other than consequences must deal with these issues. What should be underscored, however, is that consequences alone do not alter moral judgments. In a moral situation one must always stress the unity of the actor, the act, and the intended value.

From the perspective of some types of theological ethics additional issues will be raised. Some of these arise from teachings of the Scriptures: "Man shall not live by bread alone . . ." (Matt. 4:4). ". . . the things you have prepared, whose will they be?" (Luke 12:20). "And do not fear those who kill the body but cannot kill the soul; rather fear him who can destroy both soul and body in hell" (Matt. 10:28). Consequences taken by themselves tend to make light of intrinsic values. How does one evaluate the consequences to Jesus of the cross? How does the uncalculating love of God relate to the calculating justice of men? What moral evaluation may be used in all situations where men have acted through faith, as listed in the Letter to the Hebrews (11: 1-39), and yet have not received the promise? In short, what is the relation of an eschatological ethic to the commands of the law of consequences? How does it relate to the sense of vocation of a "pilgrim people of God" who, though a minority, feel called to continue to serve him throughout the centuries? These questions cannot be intelligently answered apart from a consideration of consequences even when other norms must also be applied.

D. THE LAW OF THE BEST POSSIBLE

The complexities which are confronted in recognizing the conflict of duties and values raise the familiar problem of compromise. The law of the best possible says: *"All persons ought to will the best possible values in every situation; hence, if possible, to improve every situation."*[19] In this law we recognize four emphases: the concrete situation, the possibilities of the situation, the improvement of the situation, and the role of the best. These require a comparative judgment and decision in the light of the acknowledged highest good. But they also demand ideals which are highest in the sense of being best.

Brightman sometimes calls the law of the best possible the melioristic law. It demands a critical selection, improvement, and creation of values. It has both a heightening and a moderating effect, since it points to compromise and to the highest good at the same time. It may be called the law of the uneasy conscience. It says that duty, both subjective and objective, comes to a focus in what is practically possible. The term "best" does not refer to any single value; it refers to the application of the whole system of values in conformity with the moral laws. Here the issue of the hierarchy of ends or the realm of values is again crucial.

The law of the best possible is sometimes stated in confusing and paradoxical ways. Reinhold Niebuhr has written: "Men are never committed religiously to a cause until they regard the cause as great and absorbing enough to claim their entire psyche and life. But we are confronted with the interesting paradox that no cause in human history deserves this kind of commitment, in the judgment of the faithful, if it does not pretend to be more absolute and universal than it really is."[20] What is needed, we may observe, is a religious faith which seeks to attain the most universally valid values in history, but always qualifies its devotion to these values by a sense of their relativity and partiality. Though Niebuhr regards the resolution of this problem as possible on a religious rather than a philosophical plane, it is clear that much of his writing is a theological application of the law of the best possible. His ethical perspective is often confused by the fact that he does not keep clearly in mind the distinction between non-moral and moral uses of the term "sin" in dealing with human behavior. Sin is non-moral when it is not related to the law of autonomy but is heteronomous.

The laws which have thus far been analyzed point to the fact that there is an ultimate right and wrong to every situation despite the difficulties, confusions, perplexities, ambiguities, and compromises which objectively inhere in the situations. When a person has conscientiously done what is best under the circumstances in which he finds himself, when a person is assured that the course he is following is the one obligatory upon him, he is free from moral blame even when he is in fact mistaken.[21] Even the saint must make choices of objective compromise.[22]

No contemporary moralist has stressed so emphatically and constantly the ambiguities and relativities of history as Reinhold Niebuhr, but he does not always make clear:

(1) when he is referring to the compromises forced upon us by society,

(2) when he means the conditions and limitations of finitude of the self in all situations whatever,

(3) when he is speaking of judgments due to the age in which we live, our cultural involvement, or

(4) when he is including in his evaluation the alleged perversion of conduct due to selfishness which infects all human conduct.

Since, however, he stresses not only the relativities of history but also man's responsibility for making discriminating judgments and decisions, it appears that he does, in fact, appeal to the law of the best possible. He believes that the best has positive relations to what is possible in human nature. He stresses the indeterminate possibilities of human nature in seeking the best. This is clear from a passage like the following: "The *agape* of Christ is not arbitrarily imposed upon life. It is 'from the beginning'; that is, it is given in the essential and created nature of man, which involves a freedom for which love is the only law."[23] "*Agape* is thus, as the final norm of the self as free spirit, a perpetual source of judgment upon every other norm which may be used tentatively to describe the self's duties and obligations."[24] Niebuhr thus joins the great tradition of those moralists who have never finally contended that man has a moral obligation to do something which does not lie within his powers. Like Brightman and most moralists he also finally grounds values and obligations upon the essential nature of man.[25] Man, of course, must not be isolated from his social and cosmic context. Also like Brightman, Niebuhr stresses the fact that compromise in the light of the ideal is always a provisional or present decision; for the moral law commands: "if possible, improve every situation."

Of itself the law of the best possible does not prescribe the content of the Christian ethic. It does, however, command the best and hence the consideration of all claims regarding the highest good. Accepting for purposes of discussion the Christian ethic, we can indicate more fully the nature of compromise for Christians in harmony with this law. A recent ecumenical document states the situation clearly: "The Christian will neither abstain nor conform. He will not surrender to the world, for he has already surrendered himself to God. He will not abstain because his faith calls upon him to serve God through engaging in the processes of decision and not in remaining aloof from them. He cannot discover what response to the will of God requires until he enters the situation and deals with its tensions and alternatives. Unless he participates he cannot know the will of God in the situation, and is not qualified to pass criticism on the decision. . . . The Christian knows that social order is an indispensable requisite for the satisfactory functioning, or even survival, of society. He knows that social order is effected through power structures, the ordering and differentiating of authority in offices or roles, and the interplay of forces resulting in adjustments through compromise. He knows that in this process inequity and injustice are inevitable results. But he also knows that only in this process can constructive change take place, and that the exercise of devoted faithfulness is required to direct it to greater equity and justice. In this context compromise is not a sacrifice of devotion to Christ but the faithful exercise of that devotion in a world of sin and conflict. Compromise under God's grace is the way the Christian accepts his responsibility to God and enters into the social processes."[26] This statement is admirable both in its philosophical and theological aspects.

Such a statement anticipates both the law of specification and the law of ideal control. It may leave the impression that the Christian faith is a formal framework or structure of relationships with no definitive content to point the direction which equity, justice, faith, and love will take. This may seem a weakness, but it does clarify the relation of duty to compromise.

E. THE LAW OF SPECIFICATION

As the law of the best possible is a law of relativity, so the law of specification is the law of concrete relevance. It states: *"All persons ought, in any given situation, to develop the value or values specifically relevant to that situation."*[27] This is the principle involved in Richard Baxter's admonition in *The Christian Directory:* "Prudence is exceedingly necessary in doing good, that you may discern good from evil, discerning the season, and measure, and manner, and among divers duties, which must be preferred. . . . watchfully and resolutely avoid the entanglements and diverting occasions by which the tempter will be still endeavoring to waste your time and hinder you from your work."[28]

It is not always self-evident which values or norms are most specifically relevant in situations of moral decision and action. This law is a corrective against abstract laws, against mere idealism. It is a law that recognizes the unique and unrepeatable in social process. In Chapter II this aspect of Troeltsch's view of historical wholes was incorporated in the theory of persons-in-community. "In the end," says Joseph Fletcher,[29] "all ethical issues are concrete. We have to say yes or no to existing choices; we cannot judge in the abstract." This demand is complementary to the point which Mandelbaum makes: "the concept of fittingness is the basis upon which we judge the morally relevant value of an action."[30] The value which we attribute to the action does not reside in any one of its aspects but in the fact that the actor, under the given circumstances, sets himself to perform a specific action.[31] When we judge an action to be obligatory, it is not the stronger of two demands that is decisive. What is decisive is the action "which is a fitting response to what we take to be the dominant element in the total situation which we face."[32]

The law of specification forbids escape from existential decision. All too often ethical theory is "idealistic" in the sense of dealing with good-in-general. Too often the ideals and duties seem very abstract and the moral virtues perfectionistic, without sufficient relation either to the concrete problems of conscience or to the predicaments of individual and group circumstance. Lofty ideals may distract men from present duty. Without a bill of particulars, the moralist may be irresponsible and utopian. Without obedience to the law of specification, persons in Christian churches, synagogues, lodges, service clubs, and the like easily embrace "false religion," which is what John Macmurray calls embracing ideals without concrete commitment to action.

Ideals become evils when they are substituted for action. Much of the criticism of Reinhold Niebuhr against pacifists, for example, is really a charge that they are not loyal to the law of specification. Much of the criticism of pacifists against Reinhold Niebuhr is that he is a general champion of the ethics of responsibility in concrete situations but does not actually apply the ethics of the gospel to history. He separates too radically the meaning of history and the suprahistorical norm. The law of specification is a two-edged sword. Do Christians who adhere to an ethics of responsibility accept the specific duties of their vocation as members of the pilgrim people of God?

It is also a pluralistic law, since it stresses specific duties in concrete situations. Together with all the other laws it points to an organic pluralism in the realm of morals. We have already noted how concrete duties require compromise. But past compromises are easily elevated to the status of precedents, policies, and even practical principles. Yet the best possible in each situation will be to some degree a *different* or a *unique* value or group of values. History defies general necessities, as Troeltsch so brilliantly taught.[33]

The insight which this law lifts up is appealed to in a system of ethics like that of Emil Brunner which allegedly opposes it and all principles. In *The Divine Imperative,* he takes a negative view of philosophical ethics, for obedience to God's will requires but one thing: love of God as expressed in love of one's neighbor. What are our duties to our neighbor and how do we determine them? Brunner says that we cannot be guided by any "principle" in such a situation. The content of our obligation must be discovered anew in each situation by listening to the voice of the Spirit.[34]

There is no principle that can determine in advance what love requires in a specific moral situation. Brunner is using the term
"principle" in a different sense from that of moral law as here
employed. He means some concrete maxim regarding property,
war, politics, or some ideal like equality or justice. But even love
must be expressed relevantly. The philosophical law of specification shows that the demands of love, or any other ideal, require
the special principle of paying attention to the concrete values
peculiarly relevant in a situation, in harmony with the whole system of moral laws. Brunner's error is not in his positive insight. If
we come to a particular situation with principle only, and are not
sensitive to the unique claims of the neighbor in that situation, we
may sacrifice the good of the neighbor to the principle. But this
truth is itself a principle. Brunner's error is in failing to see the
rational or philosophical law to which he has appealed. He also
lacks the ethical "ought" which requires technical empirical competence.

The law of specification points to the multiplicity of duties and
roles in modern life. It points also to changing roles. Thus it
should be clear that in a very real sense being a Christian may
have different concrete meanings for the same Christian in different situations and for all Christians in the same general situation.
There are diversities of gifts and needs to be taken into account.
To many this proposition may appear scandalous, but it is un-
avoidable. Taken alone, however, pluralism might result in expediency. This law must therefore be seen in the light of the
whole system of moral law.

Some typical illustrations will emphasize the importance of
uniting plurality and wholeness, or fittingness. One need only
consider the problems generated by (1) the division of labor in
society; (2) the multiplicity of institutions; (3) the range of co-
ercive means which are employed legitimately to maintain social
order; (4) the interpenetration of standards and techniques of
"advanced" and "underdeveloped" peoples; (5) the conflict of
interests which press in upon persons in governments. One need
only consider these to realize the need for both general policy and
concrete decisions. To isolate one issue is not morally coherent.

We may also illustrate the point by an appeal to roles. The president of the United States, the president of a university, the president of a bank, the president of a labor union, and the president of a council of churches will all have different choices to make in a national crisis, even when guided by a common ideal.

To find one's concrete duty may require extensive study. Where, for example, does one begin in the eradication of racial discrimination? What subordinate principles are involved and what methods may be employed? Here the work of the social scientist will be helpful. In his famous analysis, *An American Dilemma*, Gunnar Myrdal pointed out that prejudice and discrimination had a rank order involving (1) sex relations and family life, (2) courtesies and social respect, (3) public services and facilities, (4) political relations and institutions, (5) legal and court procedures and decisions, and (6) a host of economic relations. The analysis by Myrdal has prompted programs of action with a particular design. With the Supreme Court decisions requiring desegregation of the schools and outlawing discrimination in transportation, specific behavior in many communities has been modified. The civil rights revolution has followed no one orderly or logical course, though on the whole the movement has sought to bring state and local law into line with federal constitutional law. The hierarchy of its ends has not been consciously planned to follow Myrdal's or any other rank order. The revolution has shown that finding the means specifically relevant to a situation is as much a problem as the ends in each concrete case. R. M. MacIver has shown that the attack on prejudice should wherever possible be associated with specific programs of institutional and economic change such as can register any advance made in the moral or ideological area. Institutions tend to perpetuate themselves, affecting in time both men's habits and their attitudes.[35] To know one's concrete duty is thus by no means self-evident from a knowledge and love of only general goals and norms.

An attempt to develop a theory of responsible action in relation to a specific event has been made by Harold W. Garman in relation to the participation of Boston clergymen in the famous March on Washington, August 28, 1963. The relation of moral law theory to doctrines of the responsible self and Christian contextualism and the need coherently to relate these to social theory are brilliantly developed in his research.[36] He found, among other things, that many of the clergy had not thoroughly considered a sufficiently broad range of consequences, and they had not made a realistic and coherent reappraisal of the action in which they had participated. This reflected badly both on their motives as supposedly responsible persons and on their competence as moral leaders.

F. THE LAW OF THE MOST INCLUSIVE END

The dangers in ethical pluralism such as expediency, immediacy, provincialism, localism, exclusiveness, institutionalism, and absorption in practical-mindedness are corrected by the law of the most inclusive end: *"All persons ought to choose a coherent life in which the widest possible range of value is realized."*[37] This principle goes beyond the general axiological law in demanding a life plan for the person and an overall strategy for social action. The good life is coherent not only in cross-sectional terms or in one situation, but in terms of the whole time-span of life. The demand of the law of the most inclusive end brings the various acknowledged ideals noted in the law of autonomy into harmony. It does not repudiate the plurality of the values envisaged in the law of specification nor the fact of compromise, but it does require wholeness in the life plan. It is limited by the law of the best possible in not demanding absolute unity. It anticipates all the personalistic laws, but is placed among the axiological laws because it deals with the organization of values.

This principle, together with the other laws, calls to attention some special empirical aspects of the moral life. It recognizes the problems which arise in the varieties of wants and abilities of different individuals. While it emphasizes the abundant life, it also is aware that people have different talents. How shall a person come responsibly to terms with his potentialities? We have already noted that he must do so autonomously. For example, no one should enter a particular profession simply because his parents want him to. Heteronomous control at this point would violate the moral essence of man. No one can abdicate the responsibility for his own moral development. Herein resides one of the great ethical foundations for a free and responsible society. Yet social structures and personal vicissitudes and the consequences of early life decisions and habits enter in to set objective and subjective limits to what can be chosen. The law of the most inclusive end recognizes that freedom is limited by available alternatives.

There is a tendency for persons to follow excessively a bent or an interest and thus to grow lop-sidedly. Pedagogy sometimes violates the principle of wholeness by an excessive concentration on the child's immediate interest. But personality is more than an interest or a whole bundle of interests. It is by its nature wholistic.

There is in society the need for persons to specialize. In the communitarian laws we shall have to take account of this issue more fully. To specialize means to say "yes" to certain acts and "no" to others. However, it is whole people who should become specialists. That is why a general education should precede a more limited professional education. Throughout life it is important to enrich experiences by cultivating types of value which absorption in specialized work tends to neglect. A life plan must itself be obedient to the ideal of the most inclusive end. There must be place for new ventures, imagination, reconsideration of vocational goals, consideration of hobbies, and all that deepens and ennobles experience.

Quite frankly it must be noted that the type of ethic which emerges from the laws thus considered is perfectionist and defined by self-realization. Specialization and variety, concentration and breadth, individual and social development are all included. These are to be sought for in each person, not simply in the community as a whole. It is not enough that the community have a many-sided development and thus appear, as in Plato's *Republic,* to be whole. Persons are not simple parts of social wholes or means to social ends. Not only society but each member should be whole. So far as possible all persons should have life plans that are whole, subject to constant revision and correction. What is envisaged is adaptability and perfectibility.

We are already anticipating the law of personality. Here we

may note that a life plan or life goals steadily sought give rise to a profile of emphases on certain virtues. Virtues are the habits of willing in a person with respect to ideal goals. The ancient Greek character was stamped by certain virtues. In Plato's ethic temperance, courage, wisdom, and justice were emphasized. In Aristotle a richer variety, which included these, added high-mindedness or greatness of soul as a crowning grace. Then there was friendship, which sprang from shared perfection and devotion to virtue, a life lived in a community of excellence and generosity. The highest perfection of the soul was in the theoretic life. "Perfect happiness is a contemplative activity. . . . The activity of God which surpasses all others in blessedness must be contemplative; and of human activities, therefore, that which is most akin to this must be most of the nature of happiness."[38]

Other life plans of the Greeks included an emphasis on contentment, as in Epicurus. There was a studied concern in Epicurus to attain freedom from pain, from fear and uneasiness. This meant the avoidance of social and public involvements. In loyalty to what was "natural" the Epicurean did not champion justice, which to him was merely "conventional." Then there were the Stoics who envisioned a rational mastery of life leading to serenity. Moral conduct is man's conscious participation in a rational world-order. For the Stoic virtue is philosophy in action. But this means adjusting one's life to all-pervading necessity. It means also the victory of wisdom over the passions. "For freedom is secured not by the fulfilling of men's desires, but by the removal of desire."[39] It means an indifference to those externals over which we have no control. It means resignation.

In some early Christian ethicists the life plan of virtue attempted to adjust Christian goals to Greek ideals. Thus to Clement of Alexandria, while love is the source of virtues, moderation, temperance, and reason also play a large role: "Self-control, abiding ever, makes the man lord and master of himself; so that the Gnostic is temperate and passionless, incapable of being dissolved by pleasures and pains."[40] Augustine defined virtue as "nothing else than perfect love of God" and interpreted the fourfold Platonic pattern of virtue as four forms of love. "Temperance," he said, "is love keeping itself entire and incorrupt for God; fortitude is love bearing everything readily for the sake of God; justice is love serving God only, and therefore ruling well all else, as subject to man; prudence is love making a right distinction between what helps it towards God and what might hinder it."[41] Aquinas took the cardinal virtues of the Greeks and added to them faith, hope, and charity. He saw virtue as a "settled disposition of doing good," thus combining will and reason. The cardinal virtues are rooted in man's natural powers, and the specifically Christian or theological virtues are God's endowment of man through revelation and the sacraments of the church.[42]

Other lists of virtues could be readily supplied. For our purposes it suffices to point out that a concrete plan of life carries with it not only attention to values to be achieved in a most inclusive way but also a corresponding character pattern. The pattern of character is based both on the law of autonomy and on ideal values chosen. The total life of virtue produces a habitual attitude toward life. If virtue can be defined as "a relatively permanent attitude of will in fulfillment of obligation"[43] or a steady habit of the will in choosing the good which it acknowledges, then character as the interpenetration of the virtues reflects whatever range of values is chosen. It raises the question of what kind of personality ideal one ought to pursue.

G. THE LAW OF IDEAL CONTROL

"All persons ought to control their empirical values by ideal values."[44] Moral experience depends on personal control. This law summarizes the axiological laws and explicitly relates the experience of value to ideals. Moral ideals as here used mean criticized standards or coherent norms. The term "ideal" may be used to designate simply the definition of any type of value-claim, whether the claim be warranted or not. Empirical values must be criticized. Consequences must be evaluated. But norms too must be controlled by ideals. Ideals must be coherent. Thus at the conclusion of this chapter it is well to summarize and emphasize the significance of ideals. "Whenever we feel an obligation to ourselves," says Mandelbaum, "we are viewing some particular action

as obligatory because of its relation to an ideal which we espouse.
. . . If I merely wish to work, or to be sociable, or to be alone, I
do not feel it to be a duty to do so; the fact of obligation emerges
when some ideal stands threatened, and it is the ideal, not my
present interest, which places the demand upon me."[45]

Without subjective interests or desires there is no experience
of value; without ideal control there is no moral judgment. Emotions enter, of course, into moral judgment but not as the primary
normative consideration. Emotions lend a qualitative flavor to
judgments and affect the estimate of the shade or degree of rightness and wrongness. What some regard as a fitting object of
moral hatred others may find contemptible, and yet others as
merely morally wrong.[46] Control by ideals therefore requires self-
criticism of both thought and emotion. On the other hand, not all
ideals are norms. Knowledge of ideals is no more moral than a
definition of a dinner is a square meal. Ideals which have been
criticized, acknowledged, and chosen guide the moral life in fulfilling the possibilities of spirit. Thus the law of ideal control
implies a rejection of logical empiricism which says that men, to
the extent that they yield themselves in any considerable number
to ideals, literally determine these to be ideals in that very yielding.[47] Ideals, on this basis, are the creatures of human needs,
hopes, and aspirations. They are whatever satisfies human desires
in the largest and most general way. This psychological form of
speaking falls short of essential moral criteria.

If the position of logical empiricism is wrong, what shall be
said of absolute ideals or of "impossible possibilities"? Brightman
persistently contends that "unless what ought to be really ought
to be and to some extent *can be,* its ought is as empty a gesture
as was ever made by a marionette."[48] Spiritual life in man is a
field of contending forces, and ideal purposes are never fully in
control of consciousness. The potential energies of our hidden
powers must become active energies under the control of ideals.
Does this rule out the function of absolute ideals? Morris R.
Cohen tries to show how such ideals have a significant place in
controlling moral experience and does so without negating the
force of such an argument as Brightman's. "The recognition of

unattainable ethical ideals gives direction to our efforts and prevents our conduct from sinking back into its animal origin. But the recognition that no actual temporal act can fully embody the ideal saves us from the idolatrous worship of some particular, which no matter how good, blocks the road to something better."[49] Cohen here assumes the distinction between the ideal which beckons thought to growing perfection and the ideal which functions at the point of present moral obligation.

The concept of an "impossible ideal" has in recent Protestant thought been the occasion of considerable confusion. Unfortunately it has not been carefully defined. It may mean an ideal which cannot now be fulfilled but which can be reached in the future if we discharge our obligations now. Such future duties are preferably not called impossible.

An ideal may be impossible in the sense that we are ignorant of its nature or full content. But here the task is one of becoming more and more enlightened. It is a reminder of our fallibility. At the same time failure to do one's duty because of inability to discern the real nature of a duty is not blameworthy in the strict moral sense. However, we have an obligation to become as enlightened as possible.

An ideal may be impossible in that it abstracts from present conditions and presents a conception of a situation which could conceivably be ideal under other circumstances. This is the impossibility of utopian schemes. But utopian ideals are not the standard of moral guilt or merit.[50]

An ideal may be impossible from a human point of view but may be used to refer to the perfect union of perfect intention and perfect realization of good in God. Jesus said, "You, therefore, must be perfect, as your heavenly Father is perfect." But he never held men to be blameworthy because they were not good in this sense. In this absolute sense he repudiated the idea that he himself was good and said the idea applied only to God (Matt. 19:16-17). There is accordingly a vast moral difference between saying "You, therefore, must be perfect, *as* your heavenly Father is perfect" and "You shall love your neighbor *as* yourself."

Perfect love has been called by Reinhold Niebuhr an "impossible possibility."[51] This phrase is as contradictory as a round square. What he seems to have meant is that all moral achievements are judged in the light of the divine nature; that love is never fully embodied in any human motive or human action; that it is nevertheless relevant; and that in humility it can be approximated. The frame of reference here shifts back and forth from heaven to earth in the concept of man's standing under the judgment of perfect love. Niebuhr's maxim on "impossible possibility" seems also to confuse general observations on man's mixed motives, judgments about every single moral decision, specific obligations involving love, life-long obligatory quests to love God wholly, proximate judgments, and ultimate goals. These distinct elements can be intelligently discussed without the paradoxical phrase "impossible possibility."

The law of ideal control points to a perfectionism which is not static but which calls for fulfillment of the good in an ever increasing measure throughout life. Perfection means indefinitely realizable perfectibility.

The relation of this law to the decisions of Christians in complex situations such as in foreign policy and diplomacy may be illustrated by the observations of G. F. Kennan and H. Butterfield. Kennan writes: "I can testify from personal experience that not only can one never know, when one takes a far-reaching decision in foreign policy, precisely what the consequences are going to be, but almost never do these consequences fully coincide with what one intended or expected. This does not absolve the statesman of his responsibility for trying to find the measures most suitable for his purposes, but it does mean that he is best off when he is guided by firm and sound principle instead of depending exclusively on his own farsightedness and powers of calculation."[52] This principle is complemented by the observation of Butterfield: "Precisely because he can hold fast to spiritual truths —not turning any mundane programme or temporal ideal into the absolute of absolutes—the Christian has it in his power to be more flexible in respect of all subordinate matters, and to ally himself with whatever may be the best for the world at a given moment."[53]

VI
MORAL LAWS:
THE PERSONALISTIC ASPECTS

The moral laws are imperatives which reason discovers in moral experience taken as a whole. The experient is the person. He is the concrete actor who finds himself in a complex environment, at once interpersonal and nonpersonal in its dimensions.

There have been many efforts to define personality. It is difficult for the experient of the life of value and obligation adequately to define himself. We might say with Berdyaev that "the entire world is nothing in comparison with human personality, with the unique person of a man, with his unique fate . . . It is possible for man to get knowledge of himself from above or from below, either from his own light, the divine principle which is within him, or from his own darkness, the elemental subconscious demonic principle within him." "When a person enters the world, a unique and unrepeatable personality, then the world process is broken into and compelled to change its course, in spite of the fact that outwardly there is no sign of this."[1] The person lives in dynamic interaction with his total environment, but he cannot be defined by the environment, for environment is known through the person. This is not to question that personality is involved in the causal nexus of its world or that the content and "shape" of his experience are not dependent on many factors. But the person, the subject of moral and all other experience, is himself conscious experience.[2] The moral laws are not self-existent entities. They are moral demands within personal existence, as Brightman insists. "What is not, never has been, and never can be a person's experience is no part of him, no matter how important it may be to him. The person is what he experiences himself to be."[3] The only direct experience we ever have is our own consciousness. "All the evidence for nature, society, or God that we have or ever could have is to be found in each self, in his personal being as experience. Nature, society and God, as well as our own past and future, are all objects of belief, not of present immediate experience. The situation-experienced is not identical with the situation-believed-in." Brightman is no solipsist, as has been shown in the discussion of person and community. The situation-believed-in is a real situation whether it is fully understood or not. "To suppose that he is actor without being interactor, that he is personal without being interpersonal, or that he is an experient unaffected by his environment, is to suppose the fantastic and incoherent dream of solipsism, which is paralleled by the behavioristic theory that objects-believed-in exist, while there is no conscious observer or believer—no situation-experienced."[4]

A definition of personality in terms of experience is essential to an understanding of the moral laws of personality. The personal experient is a value. A person is dissatisfied with his experience when he cannot approve it. He seeks better experience. Since he is endowed with reason and can find rational norms, he is dissatisfied with values that are not coherent with coherent norms. Values are of, by, and for persons. "Personality is taken to be an intrinsic value; without respect for personality all other values are corrupted. Without personality, no other values exist. Unless personality is valued, all else is devalued. This principle underlies democracy, sound education, and true religion. It appears in the maxim, 'Thou shalt love thy neighbor as thyself.' "[5] When Fletcher argues that "only one thing is intrinsically good, namely love," he defines it in terms of integral personality.

A. THE LAW OF INDIVIDUALISM

The three personalistic laws—the law of individualism, the law of altruism, and the law of the ideal of personality—must be understood together in an interpenetrating whole. The law of individualism says: *"Each person ought to realize in his own experience the maximum value of which he is capable in harmony with moral law."*[6] The person has duties to himself because he is the subject who acknowledges and decides with respect to all obligations and values. The law of individualism is not a self-centered, selfish, or introverted principle. It is a norm of construction and first-person responsibility. This idea, again, has been illuminatingly expressed by Berdyaev: ". . . personality must construct itself, enrich itself, fill itself with universal content, achieve unity in wholeness in the whole extent of its life. Personality is not made up of parts, it is not an aggregate, not a composition, it is a primary whole. The growth of personality, the realization of personality certainly does not mean the formation of a whole out of its parts . . . The form of personality is integral, it is present as a whole in all the acts of personality, personality has a unique, an unrepeatable form, Gestalt."[7]

The law of individualism affirms ethical assertion, acknowledging duties to the present self and to the future self. As a pluralistic principle of human dignity and self-realization, it opposes tight collectivism. The principle is sometimes presented as "enlightened self-interest" and regarded as an eminently sensible idea; but enlightened self-interest is morally ambiguous. We must ask: By what standards is the self enlightened? Are these standards adequate to the real needs of the person? Are they complete in stating the relations of the person to the community?

The law of individualism stresses maximum value, but it adds "in harmony with moral law." To maximize satisfactions may mean only to increase pleasure quantitatively. The real point is that stressed by George F. Thomas: "The primary aim of moral action is to realize not the *greatest quantity* of values, but the values *most appropriate* for the persons whose needs one is seeking to serve. My duty is to aim, not at the *maximum* of value which could conceivably be attained, but at the *optimum* of value which is fitting in the situation."[8] This law requires an ideal of personality in order to be definitively complete.

Some theoretical objections may be raised in relation to this law, namely, that it is based on self-love and hence is not truly good; that it ignores the dilemmas of self-will or egoism; and that it lacks humility. Some formulations of Christian ethics define love so absolutely as an "other regarding" value that all duties to one's self are repudiated as self-centered or selfish acts. The extreme forms of this criticism are self-refuting, for if we may only love others, having no worth in ourselves, and must always prefer others in all things, the social consequences become ludicrous.

There is a great deal of evidence that if persons have never learned to love, or accept themselves, they are ill-prepared to try to love others. If by the repudiation of self-love a person is led simply to self-contempt, he has missed the point of Christian love and stewardship. "Acquaint yourselves," said Richard Baxter, "with all the talents which you receive from God, and what is the use to which they should be improved. Keep thus a just account of your receivings, and what goods of your Master's is put into your hands."⁹ Jesus accepted man's material concerns, his struggle with temptations, and his prayers for deliverance as normal parts of his religious life. These concerns Jesus directed, as the law of individualism directs them, to the highest good. The ethical teaching is not against due care for the future but against anxiety and self-preference. Righteousness is not easily achieved, but love does not require the destruction of selfhood.

The principle of personal self-realization does not ignore the dilemmas and predicaments of egoism. It presupposes the analyses of the laws of consequences and of the best possible. Persons are actors within a causal nexus. Any true light which can be shed from any form of depth or dynamic psychology on motives, intentions, projections, illusions, distortions, or perversions belongs to the self's responsibility for self-knowledge. Indeed the self must be aware of the truth contained in the opposition or war between a "law of its members" and the "law that is in its mind." If man did not have a capacity for cruelty and evil, there would be no point in his developing a system of moral laws to help him in his struggle. This struggle is a tribute to his capacity for self-transcendence, freedom, and decision. But we must beware of reading all the evils of contemporary society into antecedent human nature.

The great religions of the world, especially Buddhism and Hinduism, make knowledge of the real self and the real situation surrounding selfhood one of the great objectives of life. Understanding what one takes to be the ultimate facts about the human situation and the divine setting of that situation has a direct bearing on determining the optimum values of life. On the other hand, the conception of what is valuable for persons is generally reflected in one's definition of the ultimate metaphysical situation.

One tends to read present and future hopes and doubts back into the sacred texts of the great religions. Paul Ramsey presents a good illustration of this method of thought. "The depth of sin," he says, "has to be acknowledged before reading Genesis, else it would not be drawn from there alone. Jews have this same scripture, yet Jewish thought contains no notion of man's deep sinfulness. Christians do not believe man sinful because of the account of Adam's first sin in Genesis. They first have been persuaded of man's sinfulness, and then they find the Genesis account to be something of an explanation as to *why* man is what he is."[10] Despite the difficulties in Ramsey's circular method of interpretation here, it must be acknowledged that the Bible and all the great religions of the world point to the fact that man is not the center of the world. The law of individualism demands that man find concretely where his true good lies.

Finally it may be argued that this principle lacks humility. It allegedly would not provide for self-sacrifice, for the renunciation of life, for the supreme goodness of Jesus Christ who chose to die for others. But this objection misses the point of the law, which has to do with quality of life, not quantity of satisfactions. Humility requires self-knowledge and self-criticism, which are prerequisite to self-realization. Moreover, self-realization and self-sacrifice are not opposing ideas. Indeed there is much evidence that the higher forms of self-realization are possible only to those who have learned the disciplines of self-sacrifice.

It may be that a theologically false humility lies behind objections to the law of individualism on the grounds of its principle of self-assertion. God is not honored through the denunciation of his creation. God is present in his creatures, and he is glorified through the moral striving of his children. A humble temper of mind, grateful to God, and aspiring to all the good that man can realize belongs to the person whose conscience is enlightened.

B. THE LAW OF ALTRUISM

The law of altruism puts into action for other persons the obligation which the law of individualism imposes on each. As stated by Brightman the law says: *"Each person ought to respect all other persons as ends in themselves, and, as far as possible, to co-operate with others in the production and enjoyment of shared values.*"[11] This law seems to entail two distinct moral principles, altruism and co-operation. As restated by DeWolf, the law of co-operation is placed under the communitarian laws. We shall consider it there where it properly belongs. It should be remembered however that Brightman placed a high estimate on shared values and on the principle of deliberate co-operation as well as natural interpersonal experience in community life.

Altruism of the right kind must find its place in the communitarian laws, for its context is the reciprocity of human needs and interests, common needs and common goals. The value of a valid altruism is not in caring for others instead of oneself, to the positive neglect of oneself—but in self-identification with the wider claims, needs, and values of other persons. There are times when one must be prepared to "lay down his life for his friends," but this profound love is not a principle of social policy whereby one serves humanity at the expense of duties, for example, to the family.

In discussing the law of individualism we have already noted the perverse notion that all we are here for is to serve others. The elementary response to this is naturally: What are the others for? Such "altruism" or "love of the neighbor" is not the suitable antidote for selfish interest. A businessman, for example, may have service to the community as his motive; but he will not succeed in his altruistic purpose unless his business survives and remains solvent, and this means paying suitable attention to it. On the other hand, there may come times when he must surrender business success in recognition of the larger good of the community. Both utter self-interest and utter other-interest are not only contrary to human nature but ethically self-refuting positions. Moreover, the altruism which is completely devoid of concern for the person who is outgoing, plays into the hands of those who are willing and able to take advantage of, manipulate, and even destroy him in the interest of some cause. In a truly communitarian context the rights and obligations of all are co-ordinate. Even when love is made the ultimate principle, it does not void humanity as a society of intrinsic values, of persons as ends in themselves.

Paul Ramsey makes a good point when he insists that human rights are not claims which a man makes as the condition of his reluctant participation in social concerns. "A person's primary relationship to the various communities of which he is a member is one of service and not first of all one of making demands upon them. Rights do not inhere in the isolated, 'natural' individual."[12] Yet Ramsey goes too far in giving the primacy to love of the neighbor and to service when speaking of rights, for there really are claims of elementary self-respect which are not derivative from service. He is mistaken in the following illustration: "Marian Anderson has a right to sing in the Metropolitan Opera, not for Marian Anderson's sake as a private self, but for the sake of a better opera association and for the sake of Marian Anderson as a contributor to the operatic art."[13] Ramsey should have made the intrinsic worth of personality and its claim for recognition and right to participate more explicit. Respect for the intrinsic rights of persons is not self-centeredness as he seems to think. Here the deontological must have priority over the teleological value.

The proof of the law of altruism is found in an impartial generalization of the law of individualism: "if each person ought to respect himself as a realizer of value, then each person ought to respect all others as realizers of value and so as ends in themselves."[14] This type of proof echoes in part Kant, who regarded his categorical imperative as a theoretical statement of the Golden Rule, reflecting in his rational principle the powerful influence of Jesus Christ on Western altruism. Kant's famous formulation was: "Act so as to treat humanity, both in thine own person and in that of every other, always as an end and never merely as means."

A question which the law of altruism does not settle is: what values in others are to be promoted? The moral laws provide no legal code or automatic cultural content for the realization of the lives of others any more than for one's self. But adherence to the law of altruism saves the actor from subtle temptations to wish to run or manipulate the lives of other people. It is a principle of respect for all persons, hence a principle of democratic interaction. It also repudiates manipulation of persons even to assure the good of others. On the contrary, it repudiates a laissez-faire attitude in the sense of acquiescence in either majority or minority group indulgences. In conjunction with the other moral laws it invites both community criticism and realization. It recognizes both plurality of interests and responsible involvement in common ends.

The ideal of altruism needs to be related explicitly to the ideals of justice and of love; for altruism is both a principle of justice, since it directs respect to persons, and a principle of love, since it directs the will to seek the whole need of other persons as one's own. We have already noted that love and justice are not independent norms. Niebuhr contrasts what he calls "sacrificial love" from "mutual love," though not as sharply as his critics have assumed.[15] Niebuhr wishes to distinguish between the love which is, and which is not, reciprocated and "historically justified." This he does in the interest of protecting the New Testament ethic from becoming a prudential ethic, one constructed for self-regarding purposes or for ulterior ends. This caution or protest is a significant one. The meaning of love is not exhausted in the maxim that we should love our enemies because this will make them no longer our foes. The fruits of love are not to be simply equated as the assured consequences of purposive loving. The fact that people generally respond in kind to love does not guarantee that they will. Hence love is not exhausted by the calculation of success. The principle of altruism, therefore, goes beyond the element of reciprocal justice which is included within it.

Love also goes beyond justice from another perspective, which may be illustrated by Brunner's treatment of this subject.[16] Beginning with the Aristotelian principle of rendering to every man his due, he shows how a comprehensive and ultimate treatment of justice presses one to acknowledge the "heavenly justice" which returns good for evil and forgives the transgressor seventy times seven. According to Aristotle, "Only what is worthy to be loved can be an object of friendship."[17] Contrariwise, says Brunner, love asks no question about the nature of that which is to be loved. He consciously follows Nygren here. "It is a loving born simply of the will to love, not of the nature of the beloved. It is not a love which judges worth but a love which bestows worth."[18] In order to make this contrast very sharp he then says of justice:

"Justice can make no use of this love, nor does it need to. Justice is never concerned with the human being as such, but only with the human beings in relationships. Justice belongs to the world of systems, not to the world of persons. But because the person is higher than all the systems in which he is placed, because all systems are there for persons but never persons for systems, love transcends justice."[19] Justice is here abstracted from persons; yet value, as we have seen, is always a function of persons.

Brunner is in error because he defines Christian love too exclusively in terms of a person needing redemption and not as a creature whom God has made. In addition Brunner narrowly confines justice. But justice must be related to the whole person as moral agent. The moral laws are all laws of the person. New Testament scholarship has generally rejected the Nygren theses on *Eros* and *Agape* on which Brunner builds.[20] Moreover, the metaphysical problem as to how God creates worth in persons must not be confused with the problem of redemptive relationships. The great commandments of love to God and love to neighbor are not questions of conferring worth at all, but of acknowledging the Supreme Person wholeheartedly and other persons equally with one's self. Nevertheless, love goes beyond justice in its narrow sense, because the whole person responding to other persons must include their true good in the pursuit of his own. Love is comprehensive and has many aspects. Love is an inclusive ideal and law. It can also be very specific, as the law of specification points out. In the field of social policy, as we shall see, justice in the legal sense is restricted by what can apply at once to each and all, while love commands that the concrete person be served beyond the possibilities inherent in civil law. Love at once fulfills and transcends justice. When justice is interpreted in the sense of full biblical righteousness, it is akin to love.

C. THE LAW OF THE IDEAL OF PERSONALITY

The climactic personalistic moral law states: *"All persons ought to judge and guide all of their acts by their ideal conception (in harmony with the other Laws) of what the whole personality ought to become both individually and socially."*[21] This law pre-

supposes and correlates all the previous laws. It makes the unifi-
cation of value-experience, as well as the highest attainable ideal,
obligatory. Moreover, as interpreted by Brightman, it makes the
realization of the ideal obligatory both in individual and in social
experiences. The coherence of these obligations is the proof of
the law of the ideal of personality.

The unity of consciousness is an empirical datum which leads
by the implication of reflective self-criticism to the total personality. The immediate present experience is linked both to the
past and to the future. Personal consciousness is temporal. Moral
law therefore lifts up an ideal life plan, a concrete ideal of a
unified personality, to be developed as the self seeks for coherence in its journey through life from one stage to another.

As one confronts this law, one is impressed by the many concrete ideal types which have emerged in history: the philosopher-
king of Plato; the superior-man of Confucius; and the wise-man of
the Hebrews. There have been mystics, knights, contemplators,
hermit monks, crusaders, humanists, scholars, "self-made" men,
citizens, reformers, capitalists, dictators, and innumerable others
—who range all the way from the enlightened ones seeking
Nirvana to the commissars of the totalitarian regimes. The law
does not say a priori which ideal type one should choose, but it
sheds critical light on all ideals of personality. Many Christians
will point to the matchless personality of their Lord and Savior
Jesus Christ.[22] But loyalty to this law does not claim this personality as the norm in an a priori sense. Indeed it forbids the naïve
"imitation" of Christ which has often plagued the history of
Christian piety. In a deeper sense it implies a critical appraisal
of the "mind that was in Christ" as it does also of the mind that
was in Buddha, Confucius, Moses, Socrates, Muhammad, and
other leaders of world religions. The spiritual life is the system of
living realization of personal ideals. Yet the fulfillment of personality is historically concrete and individual.

The names of Jesus, Buddha, and others have a power over
men. Mandelbaum observes, quite correctly, "it is impossible to
frame a conception of an ideal balance of all virtues which would
not pale into insignificance beside the full-blooded virtue of an

actually good man."[23] Bergson recognized that the authority of great ethical and religious personality was charismatic. The good in such persons attracts acknowledgment. Kagawa, Ghandhi, Laubach, Einstein, and Schweitzer have commanded whole-response from many.

The law with which we are dealing stresses the whole person in opposition to social tendencies which make for fragmentation of individuals as functional abstractions. Men are more than roles, though the position they hold in a social system when in action indicates the roles which persons play. We have already alluded to the problem of specialization and the need of specialists. The impact of specialization and of the division of labor in human beings in modern society is persistent. The whole person goes to work. How can he remain or become whole? How, if at all, can the high degree of specialization upon which the economy rests be reconciled with the full development of human personality? Economic activity must not usurp the whole of life. Human beings must not be reduced to work or productive units. A whole culture must be planned which maintains man as an integer, so that relationships in and out of the productive realm are adequately integral. Diversity must be achieved within wholeness, and wholeness in diversity.

Some persons in revolt against the fragmentation of persons in modern urban areas look with longing eyes at the concrete ideal of personality in folk societies. But the folk society or small community situation may become intolerable in a great metropolis. It has been pointed out, for example, that if the increasing external contacts of persons in the city should be met by the same number of inner reactions as in the small town, in which one knows almost every person he meets and to each of whom he has a positive relationship, one would be completely atomized internally and would fall into an unthinkable mental condition.[24] Personality must create amidst all the perplexities of history and all the variables of social process the conditions for the realization of itself. Since personality is both product and determinant, immersed in and also transcending culture, its fulfillment calls for both personal life-plans and purposive social change.

The issue which now emerges anticipates the discussion of the communitarian laws. What a person ought to do depends on what the community ought to be. Although personality involves the principle of self-transcendence, the power of self-transcendence is limited. This ability is presupposed in rational reflection, freedom, self-control, choice, and decision. Nevertheless, character as the interpenetration of the virtues is formed within a dynamic social setting which limits and conditions selfhood. Personality types bear a positive relation to *social character*. Jesus would not have emerged in ancient Greece; Einstein would not have become what he was in rural India; Andrew Carnegie would not appear among the nomadic Bedouins. Contemporary sociology and anthropology have shed much light on character analysis in relation to cultural settings. These sciences show that self-transcendence is indeterminate, but also limited. There are significant relationships between one's experiences of growing up, one's patterns of overt attitudes to others, and even one's "world view." For example, Ephraim Rosen has given a "Self-Portrait of a Fascist."[25] Samuel H. Flowerman has presented a "Portrait of the Authoritarian Man"[26] showing that he is a supreme conformist, herd-minded, a "phoney" conservative, and a moral purist. J. C. Flügel has related father and ruler in a psycho-analytical study of the family.[27] Thorsten Veblen in his *Theory of the Leisure Class* portrayed among other things persons who were anxious for status. Karl Mannheim has argued in *Freedom, Power and Democratic Planning* that for a democratic society to develop it must nurture democratic personalities and that a society must develop certain creative characteristics and methods if democratic personalism as an ideal is to be achieved.

For students of Christian ethics the related issue arises whether the personality of Jesus Christ can be an effective power apart from a nurturing community, the church. If not, how must the church relate itself to community? There is much interest in *koinonia* ethics.

VII

MORAL LAWS:
THE COMMUNITARIAN ASPECTS

A. THE NEED FOR COMMUNITARIAN ASPECTS

At each stage in the systematic development of the moral laws, new types of empirical data have been taken into account as well as the rational requirements of consistency and coherence among the laws. Edgar S. Brightman brought his system of moral laws to a climactic conclusion in the last of the personalistic laws. In the law of altruism and the law of the ideal of personality, he made specific reference to social experience, including co-operation. His emphasis, however, was on the individual person. In the discussion of the last law the issues pointed directly to a further dimension of empirical data that involve explicit formulations of communitarian moral law if the full range of the moral situation is to be properly interpreted. The idea of communitarian laws appeals to person-in-community experience.[1]

Brightman intended that all which DeWolf has included in the communitarian moral laws be interpreted as part of the personalistic moral laws. Responsibility is first-person experience, and he was fearful that the group might be given a status that belongs properly to persons. The communitarian laws must therefore be consistent and coherent with the preceding ones.

Nevertheless, it is important to view persons empirically in social groups and processes in order to understand this final group of moral laws. These are the law of co-operation, the law of social devotion, and the law of the ideal of community. Personality is interpersonal; it is social as well as private. Groups have distinctive traits and generate distinctive problems. The principles underlying the participation of persons in groups have a bearing on moral outcomes. Genetically speaking only as selves are incorporated into and are participants in the pursuit of common interests, and subject themselves to common norms, can they develop as persons. By participation in associations and communities and by being identified through such participation, human beings become persons, aggregates become groups, and social wholes may be defined as cultures.[2]

Community life exists at many levels. There is the informal spatial community such as the neighborhood, sometimes called the symbiotic community. Such an informal community from an organizational point of view is not, however, a haphazard conglomeration of relationships but a system of interdependencies. Here the activities are co-ordinated through unconscious social forces which tend to override individual wills and intentions as, for example, in the market place. Unplanned and unregulated economic exchange determines behavior quite impersonally. Yet even spatial interdependence cannot survive unless the men who make up the community hold some common beliefs and attitudes, abide by some common standards, use at least a minimum of common symbols, and aspire to some common goals.[3] When men are aware that they share these common standards and experiences and make decisions in the light of this awareness, they comprise a moral community.

In analyzing a moral community we recognize the following:

(1) There are common or similar goals in such consciously co-ordinated efforts as winning a game, putting across a welfare drive, organizing a P.T.A., or in such personal efforts as being a good neighbor, making a success of life, or being a good sport.

(2) In addition to goals there are common procedures or rules of the game which may range all the way from mores and folkways to civil law and the conduct of a meeting.

(3) Then there are attitudes, meaning the whole responsive side of personality with respect to such things as sexual behavior, strikes, debts, segregation, and labor-management relations.

(4) Besides attitudes there are common beliefs which are verbalized or articulated interpretations of facts, such as belief in God, education, or democracy.

(5) Finally there are common symbols relating the shared goals, accepted procedures, common attitudes, and beliefs. Here language plays an enormous role.

A moral community admits of differences in intensity and kind, of participation, approval, and disapproval. There are social sanctions involved; there is a system of power and authority and accompanying feelings; and there are feelings of identification and the like.[4] These phenomena provide some of the empirical context for the formulation of all moral law but especially of the communitarian laws. Other perspectives are also illuminating, as we shall see.

One of the famous contrasts underlying much group phenomena, already noted in Chapter II, is that made by F. Tönnies between *Gemeinschaft* and *Gesellschaft*, or roughly community and association respectively. Max Weber adapted these to the terms "communal" and "associative," and his usage is commonly employed in dynamic studies of social participation. A social relationship is thus "communal" if and so far as the orientation of social action is based on a subjective feeling of the parties that they belong together. Communal relationships may rest on various types of affectual, emotional, or traditional bases. Such for example are in the family, in a religious brotherhood, an erotic relationship, personal loyalty, and a national community. In community as an ideal-type of social organization persons respond to each other as whole people and know each other well.

An "associative" relationship bases its orientation of social action on a rationally motivated adjustment of interests or a similarly motivated agreement. Such are found in a free market exchange, in a voluntary association based on self-interest, or a voluntary association of individuals motivated by adherence to a set of absolute values. Associations are generally functional organizations and have a fragmentary interest in people. Associative relationships often consist only in compromises among rival interests, the area of interest outside the compromise remaining in conflict.[5] These two types of relationship are at the basis of many conflicting and complementary goals in modern society.

B. THE LAW OF CO-OPERATION

Although communal and associative types of social experience to a degree precede reflective ethics, the moral law of co-operation raises them to the level of responsible decision. The law of co-operation states: *"All persons ought as far as possible to co-operate with other persons in the production and enjoyment of shared values."* This law commands productive participation in group life, requiring each person to seek those common values which have been referred to above as part of the moral community. Taken by itself co-operation may be either communal or associative, but the emphasis on shared values points to the community ideal. We may more fully define this ideal by referring to the discussion of community undertaken in connection with the Oxford Conference of the Life and Work Movement in 1937. Here it will be evident that the associational values are morally secondary to the communitarian ones, for without common norms and values the competition for like scarce values is socially disastrous. What, then, is community?

In *The Oxford Conference* report, community is spoken of as "primal human need";[6] as a spiritual unity;[7] as a system of social, economic, and political relationships;[8] as the church, meaning the fellowship of Christians organized in existing churches;[9] as a normative quality of group life;[10] as the national community, or *Volk;*[11] as the universal or world church;[12] as itself an "order" (*Ordnung*);[13] and as the equivalent of fellowship in a normative sense.[14] In most of these meanings community is sharply contrasted with mere association.

An association may be defined by the limited interests or purposes by which a group is constituted, as for example a trade union, a tax payers' association, a study group, a recreational club, or a professional society. Its membership is generally voluntary, and an individual may usually therefore disassociate himself from one group and join another. There are innumerable voluntary associations in a complex society or nation. They are interest-limited and functional. Participation and mutual responsibility are accordingly limited.

By way of contrast a community may be defined as a corporate society in which the whole of a people, living continuously together in one area, share a wide range of common social goals and life forms. For many people the community is the common life to which one is born, not a transient group which one chooses to join. Its ties tend to be of historic origin, not primarily of pragmatic usefulness. Its growth may be said to be natural rather than an artificial creation. Its cohesion is largely subconscious and habitual and hence tends to be more enduring than in an association. Descriptive and normative traits of community have been outlined in Chapter II.

The law of co-operation lifts the interdependence of men to the level of morally responsible participation. It does not coerce men into any one functional group, but it points up the fact that society is a moral problem and man cannot contract out of it nor may he desert it. He must work in and through groups for values which are coherent with all the moral laws. The conservation of common values may not be taken for granted. Without them a culture disintegrates. Robert MacIver notes that the myth-structure, or value-impregnated beliefs, holds society together. Each participant has a responsibility to conserve and improve the myth-structure.

Participation in social groups should be critical, creative, and responsible. This applies both to the functional associations and to the more organic communities. Through *criticism* the ends and means of the community are brought under rational review, ideals are purified, and values are made relevant to the changing scene. Through *creative* participation the unique contribution of each person is made available to the others, and the person realizes himself in the sharing. New problems are handled with the additional resources of persons who freely share in group process. *Responsible* participation refers to accountability for decisions made. Responsible persons continue to respond to each other and accept the consequences of their acts.

The law of co-operation does not envisage an equal intensity of participation by persons in any or all kinds of social groups. It points out the basic principle and points to the law of social devotion and the law of the ideal of community to complete the whole moral conception

C. THE LAW OF SOCIAL DEVOTION

As formulated by DeWolf this law states: *"All persons ought to devote themselves to serving the best interests of the group and to subordinate personal gain to social gain."* In one sense this law has already been proved in connection with earlier treatments of man and his neighbor, especially in the discussion of the law of altruism. It re-emphasizes the law of the best possible and the law of ideal control. The best interests of the group referred to in this law mean the true or adequately criticized interests of the group. Hence it is not a law of uncritical participation or devotion, but a law which carries forward what has been said about critical, creative, and responsible participation. Social devotion is a high value, but it must be constantly tempered by thorough criticism in the light of interests which go beyond those immediately entertained by the group. Group life at its best means loyalty and criticism. It means the search for the fuller meanings of personal and community life. Such meanings point to ultimate meanings— those that transcend the individual person. Persons truly find themselves only in what is best interpersonally. But the search for the best interests cannot rest until limited and partial group interests are seen in, and controlled by, the most comprehensive of all contexts: the Kingdom of God. At this ultimate level the religious and the ethical contexts merge.

The moral problem of social devotion contains many perplexing and ambiguous elements. In modern industrial urban life, for example, the tendency is to group people along associative rather than communitarian lines. A city may present the sociological appearance of being simply a large, dense, and permanent settlement of socially heterogeneous individuals.[15] But in urban society there is a physical structure, a system of technology, and spatial distribution of population. There is also a system of social organization involving a recognized pattern of social structure, a series of social institutions, a pattern of social relationships and of power. Besides, there is a set of ideas and attitudes and a constellation of personalities engaging in varying forms of collective behavior and subject to formal and informal, acknowledged and unacknowledged, mechanisms of social control. In such a society there is great differentiation of functions and services. Moreover, there develops a status system, a pattern of rank orders built on the need for maintaining unity and cohesion in the successful operation of common enterprises.

Such a society is never immune from disintegrating antagonisms, for people are here divided from one another by occupation or profession, class, and power, and as a result usually share experience only in a limited way.[16] The resultant group life may conflict with the cherished ideals of many of its participating members. Their ideals may have been formed in the small communities whose normative characteristics Brownell[17] has included in his definition. The law of social devotion commands that in each group, while subordinating personal to social gain, each member seeks to serve the best interests of the group. This law rests on the truth that each man's real self, as T. H. Green recognized, is higher than his bare individuality. It is realized only as it is devoted to all society, enveloping the whole world. He says, "until the object generally sought as good comes to be a state of mind and character of which the attainment, or approach to attainment, by each is itself a contribution to its attainment by every one else, social life must continue to be one of war—a war, indeed, in which the neutral ground is constantly being extended and which is itself constantly yielding new tendencies to peace, but in which at the same time new vistas of hostile interests, with new prospects of failure for the weaker, are as constantly opening."[18]

In the law of the ideal of community it will be noted that this devotion may mean opposition to majority or group opinion in the service of true community—hence social improvement and reconstruction. It is a principle of the sensitized social conscience at work everywhere in society. In conjunction with the law of the ideal of co-operation it is a law of both personal and social action. It may at times command revolution.

D. THE LAW OF THE IDEAL OF COMMUNITY

The climactic and summary moral law is this: *"All persons ought to form and choose all of their ideals and values in loyalty to their ideals (in harmony with the other Laws) of what the whole community ought to become; and to participate responsibly in groups to help them similarly choose and form all their ideals and choices."*[19] This is the principle of inclusive responsibility, personal and communitarian, at once pluralistic and organic. It prescribes in advance no specific pattern of culture or society. In itself it is neither centralist nor decentralist, socialist nor capitalist, and it decides for neither world federalism nor any one political instrumentation. Yet it does confirm and emphasize the supremacy of personal worth and the idea of responsible society.

This moral law must take into account the conflicting claims of associative and communal groups. Community is a more adequate ideal than association. Since community-type relationships characterize rural social organization, and urban societies are functional and associative, the conclusion is sometimes hastily drawn that rural life is superior to urban life. The assets and liabilities of small communities and associative patterns need further analysis. Moreover, these social-types tend to overlap and interpenetrate. In national and world organization ways must be found to integrate them in larger wholes. We must therefore make critical evaluations. The small community may be provincial and ensmalling, and the city may provide untold opportunities for personal development through voluntary associations of an economic, political, cultural, educational, or religious kind. In the urban world the distracting and disorganizing effects of functional differentiation and competing and conflicting groups may be seen in such phenomena as mass-mindedness, mental breakdown, delinquency, crime, suicide, corruption, and anomie. But associative groups are not properly viewed simply as disintegrative specializations which deviate from the norm of the small or rural community. Functional groups must, however, be rooted in adequate community values and oriented toward community wholeness. The moral law of the ideal of community stresses the truth that personal realization is a partnership in the good life. It raises the question of what factors are coherently present in true community.

The whole system of moral laws favors an ideal of community in which the following elements inhere: (1) organic pluralism, or human solidarity coherent with personal individuality; (2) the perspective of mankind as the unit of co-operation; (3) an understanding of cultures as wholes; (4) a concern for persons in the transformation of cultures; (5) provision for the possible continuation of a multi-group society both domestically and world-wide; (6) the possibility and validity of purposive change; (7) the preparation and implementation of fundamental human rights and freedoms; (8) the positive appreciation of religious values and norms in the life of persons and groups; and (9) the positive role of ultimate ideals. This law recognizes that cultural pluralism makes important claims; that nations are at varying stages of technical and social development; that no one "historical total-ity," to use Troeltsch's term, is normative for all others; and that varying community ideals may be specifically relative and relevant at local, regional, national, and international levels. Yet in all cases it demands purposive and responsible change.

It may be asked whether the moral command to formulate an ideal of community is not an "impossible possibility." Spinoza might have responded to such a question that "all things excellent are as difficult as they are rare." Those of us who are living in an era of rapid social change know that this moral law is difficult to obey. Yet nothing less can be commanded in harmony with the other laws, which provide for limitations of performance within the range of the possible. It may be said that the law of the ideal of community is a historical application of the theological ideal of the Kingdom of God. But the law is not an impossibility in principle. There is ample evidence that some insights regarding true community or the right social order are already operative in the social policies of nations, businesses, cultural societies, churches, and world religions. Moreover, the fact that the United Nations has its Commision on Human Rights and its Preamble to the Charter presupposes some awareness of the moral right of ideal community to control the subordinate decisions of nations, social groups, and individuals, and to provide the means for per-sonal realization. We are living in an era of conflicting power groups, rival ideologies, competing world faiths, and "cold war." A fighting faith may or may not express loyalty to the moral law of community.

As people in different parts of the world recognize world-wide symbols, ideals, and goals as their own, and give these a high

place, the sooner will they develop a world community. Margaret
Mead says, "We do not want one value system with which every-
body would identify himself in a direct line relationship, but we
want each people to realize that there is a relationship between
themselves and those symbols that might become world symbols."[20]

The law of the ideal of community expresses both the law of
the best possible and the law of the most inclusive end, as well as
the law of ideal control, and applies them to community values.
World community may be most likely achieved when the different peoples of the world strive for over-all symbolic and inclusive norms and see themselves giving allegiance to them in ways
congruent with their own cultural values. In so doing they ought
to seek to understand why and how other peoples find their re-
spective cultural values also congruent with the over-all ideal,
though diverse from their own. They must seek to find what
those cross-cultural themes and norms are which give common
substance to the daily lives of persons and groups everywhere.
The moral law of ideal community is thus coherent with "the
type of multidimensional world culture, within which there would
be interdependence of diverse values rather than a world in which
any one interest or function so dominated the others that single
value scales, competition, and destruction were the concomi-
tants."[21]

The law of the ideal of community asks not only for adequate
goals but also for responsible participation in group decision. It
asks men to confront realistically the means for achieving these
goals. There is thus not only the problem of persons being ex-
istentially committed to certain ultimate beliefs, but there is also
the question about their differences in relating ultimate beliefs to
practical policies. Some may honestly believe, for example, that
Gandhi showed the right way to use non-violent means for valid
social goals. Others may, with Gandhi, hold to the relevance of
the ideal of love to justice and yet say that Gandhi "made the
pretension of sainthood into an instrument of political power."[22]
Some will contend that a form of pacifism is the only ethic of
means coherent with the moral ideal of a community of justice

and love. Others will contend that though the love ethic is final on the one hand, it must on the other hand include "all the discriminate judgments and commitments which we may broadly define as commitments to the cause of justice" and that these may responsibly involve us at times in war.[23] Though the rightness of an ideal does not guarantee its realization, "the difficulty of its realization is no argument against it, if it is right."[24] And surely the deliberate choice of a means which is incoherent with the end sought presents serious moral difficulties. The presentation of the moral laws as a whole, I believe, provides the system of ethical reflection within which such issues must be resolved.

This law recognizes as do the other communitarian laws that society is concretely interpersonal. Social life, as Green pointed out, is to personality what language is to thought. "Language presupposes thought as a capacity, but in us the capacity of thought is only actualised in language, so human society presupposes persons in capacity—subjects capable each of conceiving himself and the bettering of his life as an end to himself—but it is only in the intercourse of men, each recognized as an end, not merely a means, and thus as having reciprocal claims, that the capacity is actualised and that we really live as persons."[25] The social life of man is historical, and this fact has tempted many to think of some historical principle over and above persons as the bearer of community ideals. Freedom, progress, and the classless society are such abstract ideas which have been urged as impersonal or superpersonal forces of history. When we recognize, however, that social values are, in Green's words, "relative to value for, of, or in a person," there can be no automatic law of value realization in society or history. Persons achieve or fail in freedom. No metalogical law guarantees success. Where the thoroughly personal character of social life is recognized, no dogmatic optimism—or pessimism—will be asserted. The predicament of man, as we noted it earlier, attends the realization of the communitarian ideal.

Yet because the foundation of society and history is personal, man must formulate and seek to realize the ideal of community. It is not a matter of indifference what form and substance the community will have. Man's moral capacity must be presupposed

in his efforts to develop the good society, but his personal fulfillment comes about only through the habits, institutions, and laws
in virtue of which men form communities, nations, and international orders. As the nation is no suprapersonal subject and has
no metaphysical status all its own, so the life of the nation becomes
an assignment in personal and social responsibility. The formulation of the moral ideal of community becomes an assignment in
developing a social environment in which persons can be realized
to an optimum degree.

From the recognition that man is a socius with a private center,
it is possible to be aware that his problems will have two foci:
those that arise from the social factors and those that arise from
within the self. The dilemmas that arise from the tensions of
these two foci must be realistically faced in dealing with the climactic moral law.

E. THE METAPHYSICAL LAW

The moral laws point everywhere beyond themselves. Choice
has a context in the whole person, the person in community, the
community in history, history in cosmic action. In addition, then,
to the formal, axiological, personalistic, and communitarian laws,
there is need, as was noted at the end of Chapter III, for a trans-
itional law standing between ethics on the one hand and metaphysics, philosophy of religion, and theology on the other. As the
ultimate context of Christian ethics reaches down for moral law
formulations in moving toward concrete choice, so these reach
upward toward ultimate context. The law says: *"All persons ought
to seek to know the source and significance of the harmony and
universality of these moral laws, i.e., of the coherence of the
moral order."* The reaching down and the reaching up is, of
course, not spatial. Ultimate dimensions and categories interpenetrate without dislodging one another.

The Christian dimension of social ethics expresses an evangelical emphasis, the centrality of Jesus Christ, the primacy of
grace, justification by faith, the supremacy of love, the Christian
koinonia, the freedom of love (*agape*) from the rigidities of legalism and codes, and the relevance of ethics for social action. The

dimension of moral law emphasizes consistency; autonomous obligation; consequences; harmony of values; the best possible; specific and relevant decision; control by ideals; the concreteness of personal wholeness in individual and altruistic love; the duty to co-operative, critical, and creative community life. Theological ethics is introduced by faith and is disciplined and clarified by reason. Philosophical moral law is discovered through reason and commands openness to faith. Both become coherently whole in rational love.

Both are involved in that tradition which forms the subject of the following chapter, the natural law as taught in the church. That tradition, so widely criticized today, has the merit of seeking to unite ultimate moral law and concrete human ends, values, and functions. However, it has the difficulty of not distinguishing sharply the specific interests and values of the church and society in various times and places from the ultimate claims which are meant by its particular conceptions of "nature" and of "law."

VIII
MORAL LAWS
AND THE NATURAL LAW

Having formulated the system of moral law which has been the objective of this book, it is the next task to show its function as an alternative to the natural law tradition. The conceptions of both the natural law and the moral laws oppose a Christian ethic which is primarily a provisional or relative contextualism. Both hold that there are laws, criteria, and objectives which make universal claims. A self-sufficient contextualism, particularly a moment-by-moment contextualism, is morally self-refuting. When, however, ethics is given a Christian context and the person is asked to relate his choices to what God is doing in the world, and when God's willing is studied as the action of the Holy Spirit developing tradition in the church and in history at large, every situation is entered into obediently and has moral content, and love is presented as having "principles and structure." The moral laws have presented rational structures of ought which show how love fulfills itself responsibly.

A. INTEREST IN NATURAL LAW

The discussion of the natural law in ethical theory has been under an eclipse in theological circles for a number of years. In many philosophical circles the eclipse is equally dark. This eclipse has been deliberate on the part of those Protestant theologians who have taken a radical christological position and in the name of biblical theology have attacked philosophical ethics. Traditionally, of course, both philosophical and theological ethics have been closely related to each other through the idea of the natural law, though in varying degrees depending on the particular definition and validation of the basic conception involved. Indeed, Christian ethical theory has been profoundly influenced by the Stoic version of the natural law and philosophical expositions of natural law have reflected many of the valuations found in the Christian faith about man, society, and responsibility.

Beginning about 1950 there has been a revival of interest in the idea both by philosophers and by theologians.[1] But differences of opinion are marked as to the advisability of reviving the term and even more about the meaning, fruitfulness, and validity of the natural law.

Theology itself is sharply divided on the sources and nature of justice, which is the essence of the principle of classical natural law. This is due to the internal conflict in theological ethics on the relation of revelation to reason. But many other issues are involved also. The strict christological perspective of Karl Barth, Jacques Ellul, and Heinrich Søe repudiates a natural moral law of justice entirely. Contemporary Roman Catholics, Anglicans such as the late Archbishop Temple, and the free churchman Sidney Cave adhere to varying forms of it. Some, like Emil Brunner, recognize an element of essential truth in it, but feel that so much confusion and ambiguity are associated with natural moral law that it is best to dispense with the use of the term. Still others, like H. Wendland, are contending for a new synthesis between the idea of the orders of creation in Christian theology and the core of natural law ethics. All these points of view, it should be noted in passing, are opposed to naturalism as an ethical theory. The ecumenical movement, which now embraces both the World Council of Churches and the Roman Catholic Church, has stimulated a revival of interest in the relation of natural theology to revealed theology, and this has in turn been reflected in renewed explorations of natural law. Such interest is also stimulated by the relationship of ecumenical church concern for a responsible society.

John Bennett, recognizing that there is today considerable difference between Roman Catholic and Protestant theologians in their attitude toward natural law, criticizes the concept as follows: "My conclusion is that the concept of natural law has become very ambiguous and, often, it is given moral content that does not at present have support of the reason or the conscience of persons outside a particular tradition."[2] Despite these difficulties he recognizes the need to find a substitute for the concept. Theologians

who attack it have often some equivalent concept. Thus Karl
Barth introduces the idea of co-humanity as belonging to the
structure of human existence itself. So also Dietrich Bonhoeffer
acknowledges that pagan governments have moral guidance in
the "providential congruity between the second table of the Ten
Commandments and the inherent law of historical life itself." He
adds: "Failure to observe the second table destroys the very life
which government is charged with preserving."[3] To Barth's and
Bonhoeffer's the name of Reinhold Niebuhr may be added. Yet,
while critical of natural law doctrine, he has criticized an early
view of Karl Barth's in the following way: "Karl Barth's belief
that the moral life of man would possess no valid principles of
guidance if the Ten Commandments had not been introduced by
revelation is as absurd as it is unscriptural."[4]

Erick Wolf in an attempt to give a fresh orientation to the discussion has analyzed the whole Western development in terms of
the two component ideas "nature" and "law."[5] He traced the dependence of the concept of natural law on the varying ideas of
nature. He also showed the dependence of the idea of natural
law on the plurality of meanings of law (*Recht*). The combination
and interpenetration of varying meanings of nature and law
(*Recht*) give to the whole subject an overwhelmingly ambiguous
aspect. Yet, while the concept has a plurality of meanings, the
function of natural moral law is specific. It grounds and delimits
all law (*Recht*). Its reality is constitutive for human existence: it
constitutes a realm (*Ens humanum*) which includes not only consciousness but also feeling and will. What this reality is is not a
priori definable; yet it is an objective estate of being which is
given prior to all possible reflection. Its intention is to be the
legitimating ground of all positive law, but it is also the normative
standard of all empirical-historical law (*Recht*). In this respect
its function is criticism as well as ground.

B. DEFINITIONS OF NATURAL LAW
AS REFLECTED IN ITS DEVELOPMENT

The principles of a natural law of justice in Greek thought go
back at least as far as Sophocles' *Antigone,* where an appeal is

made to it as an unwritten immutable law of heaven. Both Plato
and Aristotle conceived of ethics as grounded in nature, as belonging to the first principles of being. It was through the Roman
lawyers who were trained in the Stoic philosophy that the political
thought of the Greeks ultimately passed to the West. The great
jurists like Ulpian and Gaius gave to Roman law its philosophic
content. From Cicero they learned of the distinction between the
jus naturale (natural law), the *jus gentium* (law of nations), and
the *jus civile* (civil law)—the *jus naturale* being ultimately normative.

Cicero's conception of law is set forth at length in the *De
Legibus* and in the *De Re Publica.*[6] "True Law," he says, "is
right reason consonant with nature, diffused among all men, constant, eternal; which summons to duty by its commands and
hinders from fraud by its prohibition, which neither commands
nor forbids good men in vain nor moves bad ones by either. To
make enactments infringing this law, religion forbids, neither may
it be repealed even in part, nor have we power through Senate
or people to free ourselves from it. It needs no interpreter or
expounder but itself, nor will there be one law in Rome and
another in Athens, one in the present and another in time to
come, but one law and that eternal and immutable shall embrace
all peoples and for all time, and there shall be as it were one common master and ruler, the God of all, the author and judge and
proposer of this law. And he who obeys him not shall flee from
himself, and in spurning the nature of human kind by that very
act he shall suffer the greatest of torments, though he escapes
others which men consider pains."[7] Men are joined to God
through right reason, which is law and which is the foundation of
the state. "For there is one law by which the society of men is
held together, and one *lex* has established it. That *lex* is right
reason in commanding and forbidding, and one who disregards it
is unjust whether it has ever been written or not."[8] The foundation
of the state in objective justice is thus coeval with God. The *jus
naturale* (the eternal rational principle of right) did not become
law when it was written but when it was made; and it was made
at the same time as the mind of God.

The study of the state in Cicero, then, begins with a study of nature and human nature by which men are equal. All men and all races of men are capable of virtue; it is vice and wrongdoing, not nature, that produces inequality. This emphasis, Carlyle and McIlwain point out, is the most important difference between Cicero and the greatest of the Greek philosophers. It is also the "dividing line between the ancient and the modern political theory." It is the profoundest Stoic contribution to politics. Man as man shares law coeval with God, and by nature he shares it with other men of whatever race or city, and this before the foundation of any state and its enactment of a *jus civile*.[9]

The early church fathers were profoundly influenced by Stoic conceptions of the natural law, especially as expressed by Seneca. Paul's reference to the Gentiles as doing "by nature what the law requires" (Rom. 2:14) is significant in this connection. The natural law concept served the development of Christian ethics as the Logos concept served theology generally.[10] A modification of the Stoic idea occurred in the distinction between the natural moral law as absolute and the relative natural law. The latter was the embodiment of the former in human codes, and this provided a vehicle for reconciling the Christian ideal with the necessities of contemporary social life. This idea also helped to distinguish the status of the natural law in man before and after the fall of man.

An important development occurs in the conception of law in Thomas Aquinas. Here the Stoic doctrine is synthesized with the teleological ethics of Aristotle and with the hierarchical requirements of canon law, the claims of supernatural revelation, and the structure of church authority. Aquinas' essential position is normative for papal encyclicals up to John XXIII. Law, for Aquinas, is a function of reason. It "is a rule and measure of acts, whereby one is induced to act or is restrained from action. . . . The rule and measure of human acts is reason: It being the part of reason to direct to the end, which is the first principle of conduct."[11] This formulation of law seeks to combine the first principles from which rational deductions are made with the ends of ethics. These ends are placed in a hierarchical pattern of goods and interpreted by the church. Since the world is ruled by

Divine Providence, the whole community of the universe is gov-
erened by Divine Reason, and so the plan of the government of
all things has the character of law. Since each institution has its
proper end, each is given a particular status in this order of law.

Aquinas develops a fourfold pattern of law. First, there is the
"eternal law." It is nothing else than the plan of divine wisdom. It
has the character of an exemplar, pattern, or idea by which all
things are created. It corresponds quite closely to the natural law
of the Stoics, though having its setting in a different idea of God.
Second, there is what he called "natural law." This is the participation of the rational creature in the eternal law, whereby man
has a natural inclination to a due act and end. The relationship
may also be stated conversely: "The natural law is nothing else
than a participation of the eternal law in the rational creature."
Third, there is "human law." Human laws are conclusions drawn
from the natural law for the particular determination of various
matters. Fourth, there is "divine law." Divine laws are principles
for the guidance of human life in order that man might know
without a doubt what to do and what to avoid. This is especially
needed since the end of man exceeds the measure of the natural
faculties of man. "Because man is ordained to an end of eternal
blessedness, which exceeds the measure of the natural human
faculties, therefore it was necessary that, over and above natural
law and human law, he should be further guided to his end by a
law given from God."[12]

The natural law for Aquinas has a basic precept that good is to
be done and gone after, and evil is to be avoided. Other precepts
are based on this. There are three forms of these practically derivative aspects of natural law: (a) self-preservation and the appropriate positive and negative means thereto; (b) inclinations and
knowledge shared with animals, such as sexual intercourse and
education of offspring; and (c) inclinations to man's proper good,
such as to know the truth about God, to live in society, to avoid
ignorance, and to shun offending other men.[13] On the basis of his
fourfold scheme of law, Aquinas developed a grand design of
social and ecclesiastical ethics covering property, the state, the
family, labor, and the church.

In the Reformation period a major revolution in thinking about the natural law of justice was initiated. Neither Luther nor Calvin overthrew the medieval concept entirely, but they tended to identify the natural law with the divine law and especially with the Decalogue. The concept was virtually equivalent also with the order of creation. But beginning with Hugo Grotius the doctrine took a radically new turn. Grotius defined it as follows: "The law of nature is a dictate of right reason, which points out that an act, according as it is or is not in conformity with rational nature, has in it a quality of moral baseness or moral necessity; and that, in consequence, such an act is either forbidden or enjoined by the author of nature, God." He lifted up the traditional relation of human reason to natural law and made it the leading principle.[14]

The philosophers of the Enlightenment both on the Continent and in England developed a theory of the natural law of reason in opposition to the medieval synthesis and the authority of the church. With Locke it became a doctrine of individual rights (life, liberty, and property) as over against the state. At the same time the concept of nature underwent a significant shift from an order of first principles of morals to a conception of the order studied by the physical sciences. This last order then came under the conception of science, which rejected "final causes" or purpose in nature, and finally scientific law tended to mean simply a statistical description of predictable probabilities. Nature was also defined as a system of measurable laws which were completely self-contained, having no ground or basis of calculation beyond themselves. Echoes from the earlier idea of a moral order or justice lingered however, as in the Declaration of Independence: "We hold these truths to be self-evident,—that all men are created equal; that they are endowed by their Creator with certain unalienable rights; that among these are life, liberty, and the pursuit of happiness."[15] Man's natural state was the subject of confused speculation during the Enlightenment sometimes referring, as with Locke, to a supposed primitive and normative social condition; sometimes, as with Hobbes, to the necessary conditions and prerequisites of lasting peace and security; and sometimes, as with Bayle, to the axiomatic principles of the inherent goodness which sovereign reason sanctions and promulgates. There were many variations and combinations of these themes.

In the contemporary world a general ambiguity reigns in relation to the meaning of the term "natural law." Bentham's summary of this confusion is still relevant: "A defect this to which all books must almost unavoidably be liable, which take for their subject the pretended law of nature; an obscure phantom, which, in the imagination of those who go in chase of it, points sometimes to manners, sometimes to laws; sometimes to what law is, sometimes to what it ought to be."[16] The moral law of justice, we believe, is no phantom, and much clarifying thought is needed; but the task is not easy, and the outcome is not assured.

C. ROMAN CATHOLIC FORMULATIONS

The papal encyclicals on social questions by Leo XIII and Pius XI have made frequent appeals to the natural law. Leo followed Aquinas in his general formulations but tied his applications to contemporary institutional and social requirements of the church, taking an essentially conservative position. In *Libertas Humana* (1888), he notes "that the law of nature is the same thing as the *eternal law,* implanted in rational creatures, and inclining them to their right action and end; and can be nothing else but the eternal reason of God, the Creator and Ruler of all the world." Human law does for the citizens of states what reason and natural law do for men. Laws come before men live together in society, however, and have their origin in the natural and eternal law. The precepts of the natural law contained bodily in the laws of men have not the force merely of human law but of eternal law. The grace of God works inwardly in man and in harmony with man's natural inclinations, so that the eternal ends of man are under the divine and the natural laws in harmony with each other. God is the sole standard of human liberty for both the individual and the community. Therefore perfect liberty is obedience to God. The church guards and protects liberty. No man is morally free independently to decide the limits of the legislative authority of God. Indeed, the chief duty is to worship God with devotion and piety. Therefore there is no need of the "fatal theory" of separation of church and state. The role of the church, then, in determining the content of natural law becomes evident, for it interprets divine law and the hierarchy of the ends of life.

Leo's fundamental medieval conservatism from which he never departed, even in the famous *Rerum Novarum,* follows from the above abbreviated argument: "Wherefore, civil society must acknowledge God as its Founder and Parent, and must obey and reverence His power and authority. Justice therefore forbids, and reason itself forbids, the State to be Godless; or to adopt a line of action which would end in godlessness—namely to treat the various religions (as they call them) alike, and to bestow upon them promiscuously equal rights and privileges. Since, then, the profession of one religion is necessary in the State, that religion must be professed which alone is true, and which can be recognized without difficulty, especially in Catholic States, because the marks of truth are, as it were, engraven upon it."[17]

It is instructive to note some specific areas in which a substantive content is ascribed in the encyclicals to the natural law. The individual right of property and ownership must not be touched and stands inviolate.[18] Inequality among men of different powers and mind is recognized in inequality of possessions. Since every man has by nature the right to own and possess property,[19] and since man is older than the state, he has the right of providing for the life of his body prior to the state.

The family ethic of the encyclicals is grounded in the natural and primitive right of marriage,[20] and hence no human law may limit the natural end of marriage, which is to beget children. The family is a natural society anterior to every kind of state or nation and with rights and duties of its own, totally independent of the commonwealth. Hence the right of property belongs to a man in his capacity as head of a family. It also follows that there is a natural right of family inheritance. The law of nature gives the right and duty of educating the children to the family. The Code of Canon Law says, "The primary end of marriage is the procreation and the education of children."[21] It is then argued that the natural law is opposed to birth control by means of contraceptive devices. "Those who in exercising [the conjugal act] deliberately frustrate its natural power and purpose sin against nature and commit a deed which is shameful and intrinsically vicious."[22]

Civil society also is grounded in the natural law, for man's instinct moves him to live in civil society and isolated he cannot provide for himself. Since every civilized community must have a ruling authority, and this authority has its source in nature, all public power proceeds from God. Rulers possess authority solely for the welfare of the state.[23] This does not predetermine the form of government, however. Moreover, man has a fundamental right to form voluntary associations. Such natural rights the state must protect. The state is, nevertheless, an institution which is perfect in its own kind, for its ends are determined according to natural law and it is competent to exercise the means appropriate to the right temporal ends of men which are its domain.

The influence of Pope Leo XIII in grounding the social encyclicals in the Thomistic natural law method of argumentation has undergone a major shift, particularly in the two recent encyclicals of Pope John XXIII, *Mater et Magistra* and *Pacem in Terris*. This change has become quite revolutionary during the period of Vatican Council II and manifests itself not only in the sphere of religious liberty and family questions but also in the whole posture of the efforts to relate the church effectively to the social problems of the modern world. At this point the major observation is that the natural law is grounded in personality as a whole and not so analytically in the hierarchically structured functions of man's body and mind. Pope John emphasized that in the new situation with developments in the fields of nuclear energy, the production of synthetics in chemistry, automation in manufacturing and services, mass communication, modernization of agriculture, and the like, rights and freedom of the person must be redefined so as to express his basic dignity.

Vatican II provided a historic occasion for much fresh thinking about family ethics, population control, and family planning. With this has gone some vigorous reflection on the natural law. Many lay progressives argued as follows. The natural law is the fruit of reflection on man's rights and duties in his human situation. Hence the natural law is oriented toward and culminates in the fulfillment of human nature in its totality, demanding respect for the human person. Man's intervention in nature can raise delicate questions but there is a norm in the overall good of the individual and mankind. Hence intervention in the natural order is not a question of denying God's sovereignty, but of recognizing man's part in the creative process for which he has been given intelligence and will.

On the basis of this general conception it is argued that there is no possible conflict between a natural law based on respect for human values and a control of human fecundity, including the means employed to attain it, oriented toward man's total well-being. The obligation of fecundity must be seen to rest with a series of acts, with the whole of married life. The overall end of marriage is the family, and it is the total and lasting union of two people in married love that forms the basis of a truly human fertility. The sexual relationship between the partners embraces their whole human personality, and is therefore evidently an essential element in the attainment of this unity. It should be the responsibility of the partners to determine the limits of continence, even when they are faced with the need to regulate births. These progressive thinkers are in these ways convinced that a place must be found for a concept of the natural law which does not exclude man's effective responsibilities with regard to procreation.[24] The method of thinking about natural law is also involved. Professor Louis Dupre in discussing birth control says, "Only when applied to the concrete situation do these precepts of natural law become practical norms, for no moral principle can become practical before it confronts all other moral principles involved in a particular case."[25] The spirit of this comment is analogous to the method of the moral laws developed in the previous chapters above.

We may now turn from these papal encyclicals to some less official formulations of natural law doctrine. Jacques Maritain states "that there is, by virtue of human nature, an order or a disposition which human reason can discover and according to which the human will must act in order to attune itself to the necessary ends of the human beings. The unwritten law, or natural law, is nothing more than that."[26] He recognizes that many discussions of natural law give the impression of its being a ready-made code "rolled up within the conscience of each of us, which each one of us has only to unroll, and of which all men should naturally have an equal knowledge."[27] Strictly speaking, however, the only practical knowledge all men have naturally and infallibly in common is that we must do good and avoid evil. The natural law is the ensemble of things to do and not to do which follow from this common knowledge or principle in necessary fashion, and from the simple fact that man is man.[28] Since man has ends to be fulfilled in his nature as a person, the rights of man are also rooted in this natural law. Man is freely obligated. By virtue of natural law the human person has the right to be respected, is the subject of rights and possesses rights.

Maritain makes some distinctions in the field of rights not made in the papal encyclicals. He holds that the rights to existence, to personal freedom, and to the pursuit of the perfection of moral life belong to natural law. But the right to the private ownership of material goods, though rooted in natural law, belongs to the law of nations, or what the Stoics called the *jus gentium*. Moreover, the particular modalities of this right are determined by positive law (*jus civile*). Maritain's approach provides the emergent recognition of rights not noted in earlier periods because of different historical and social circumstances.

Heinrich Rommen has written a definitive treatment of natural law theory in his authoritative work *The State in Catholic Thought*. His interpretation is essentially Thomistic.[29] He is also an ardent defender of the Universal Declaration of Rights and Freedoms of the United Nations. He does not derive the foundation of these modern rights from the natural law alone but recognizes in this formulation of universal rights the explicit impact of Christianity on the West. He takes into account also other historical forces, social, economic, and political. He stresses the need of understanding church and state as independent societies, their laws differing in competencies and object, with the duties of citizens and the rights of secular authorities based on natural law and not on supernatural authority.[30] He approaches tolerance as a prudential maxim which takes into account the inviolability of consciences, the common good, and the interests of religion and public morality. He holds that even in a "Catholic" state the government has no right to violate the consciences of the religious minorities as long as their external acts do not disturb the public order. He does not hesitate to acknowledge the confusion which Catholic writers have helped produce by not distinguishing between fundamental natural law and the applications of this law made by church authorities, especially in certain periods of reaction to modern revolutionary movements.

The much debated "Declaration on Religious Liberty" at Vatican II is much closer to the thinking of Maritain and Rommen than to the classical arguments which held that error has no rights. Bishop de Smedt, in introducing the discussion in November 1963, cited four reasons for the Council to proclaim the right of man to religious liberty: (1) the question of truth; (2) the defense of mankind almost half of whom are deprived of religious liberty; (3) the concern for peaceful social life; and (4) ecumenism. By this latter point he meant that many non-Catholics "harbor an aversion against the Church or at least suspect her of a kind of Machiavellianism because we seem to them to demand the free exercise of religion when Catholics are in a minority in any nation and at the same time refuse and deny the same religious liberty when Catholics are in the majority." Bishop de Smedt defined religious liberty positively and negatively. "Positively, religious liberty is the right of the human person to the free exercise of religion according to the dictates of his conscience. Negatively, it is immunity from all external force in his personal relations to God, which the conscience of man vindicates to itself." Man's "liberty is offended when obedience to the dictates of his conscience in religious matters is impeded." In the debate which followed Cardinal Legèr of Montreal pled with the Council for an unequivocal declaration that would be applicable to all men without exception, even those who do not believe. This view was in sharp contrast with one expressed by Cardinal Michael Browne—a view which exposes the difficulties many have had with traditional formulations of the natural law—when he objected to putting the foundation of religious liberty in the rights of the human conscience. "It is evident," he said, "that social rights based on an individual conscience which is erroneous cannot be equated with rights flowing from an individual conscience which is right." In 1965 Vatican Council II overwhelmingly passed a definitive document affirming man's civil right to religious freedom.

D. DIFFICULTIES IN THE ROMAN CATHOLIC FORMULATIONS

Contemporary Protestant criticisms of natural law theories may be divided between those views which specifically attack its Roman Catholic formulations and those which deal with the basic idea. We may list some of the former as follows:

1. Natural law in the older encyclicals rests on two presuppositions: (a) that the reason employed in its formulation is pure and uncorrupt, and (b) that human nature and the forms of human society are sufficiently constant to allow of the formulation of principles which shall have a permanent validity. These are held to be questionable.[31]

2. Specifically it can be shown that the views of property and socialism in the encyclical by Pope Pius XI entitled *Quadragesimo Anno* recognizes in effect the inadequacies of *Rerum Novarum* by Leo XIII, which claimed to lay down on these points permanent and universal principles for the control of society. Hence the papal encyclicals, while appealing to natural law, seem to define its content differently. Even in *Quadragesimo Anno* reverence for tradition seems to stand in the way of a more impartial investigation of the social problem. In other words, the supposed natural law seems to be used as an instrument of conservatism rather than an objective norm. Property as possession and right of ownership gets more emphasis than the problem of property as power. But in industrial countries it is apparent that the crucial problem is not so much one of ownership as of power control in economic relations.[32]

3. The connotations of the words "nature" and "natural" in the encyclicals is not always clear. Sometimes the precepts of natural law are based on an intuition into the alleged permanent character of human nature, but sometimes they are claimed to be self-evident deductions from the primary proposition that good is to be done and evil avoided. This makes for confusion. Moreover, the doctrine of ends enters in continually to complicate the

discussion, for it is a doctrine which reflects, as usually stated, the requirements not of primordial moral law but of the theological ethics of the church.[33]

4. The content of natural law is often infused with ethical perspectives which presuppose the changing historical interests of the church.

5. The teaching on birth control confuses natural moral law and "nature." Joseph Fletcher has gone into this issue with great care and thoroughness, showing how some Catholic authorities like Father Connell state the issue: "In determining the *prescriptions* of the natural law on marriage, good and evil are *estimated* on the basis of what ordinarily or normally happens."[34] Fletcher replies to the use made of the appeal to natural law against contraception as follows: "To assert the existence of a Natural Law is one thing, but to derive its content from the incidence of physical nature, rather than from the moral insight of men, is to twist the classical Christian idea into a mechanistic strait jacket, and to deny true morality by submitting to fatality, to helpless determinism."[35]

Fletcher's criticism is now acknowledged by many Catholic laymen and moral theologians. They argue as follows: the traditional teaching of the church allows that acts can be intentionally infecund, but the method employed to ensure this absence of fecundity is only sanctioned insofar as it does not deprive the act of its procreative power. So there is a latent contradiction in every permitted method of fertility control: on the one hand the sexual act can be effectively and intentionally infertile, but on the other, its external form must still respect what is considered to be its "fertile character." In the traditional view, fertility control can be permitted only at the cost of a contradiction between the effective and intentional content of an act and its external form.

6. When used as a support for the special institutional claims of the church, the natural law instead of uniting men ethically on a common foundation divides men. This arises in part because the church claims authoritative and final knowledge of the true hierarchy of ends for men and societies. The church does not grant to the universal and rational element in the natural law the critical function which it ought to fulfill. An appeal to eternal

rational law ought in effect to have practical applications without special content being provided by the church. The divine law, which the church interprets, tends to displace in practice the independent and critical function of natural law even when the latter is appealed to. The rational principles in the natural and eternal law of justice, therefore, do not play the role of ultimate judge over cultural expressions of justice which they did in the period of the great Roman lawyers. There seems to be little evidence that natural law in the Roman Catholic Church is a principle of genuine self-criticism of positions taken by the church.

7. The Aristotelian-Thomistic system of natural law is so rationalistic an approach to justice that persons who orient their concepts of righteousness and love in the New Testament as the ultimate norms of ethics find it impossible to relate love to justice in this form or structure. Traditional natural law doctrine is thus defective in not taking into account sufficiently the freedom of man in his capacity for self-transcendence. There is no fixed structure of nature or reason or history which man does not transcend by virtue of his spiritual freedom.[36] One of the weaknesses which results from this failure to regard freedom is to use natural law theory to give sanction to historically contingent elements.[37] Another way of getting to the same point is Niebuhr's statement: "I tried to make the transcendence of love over law to mean the indeterminancy of love as against the determinate obligations which are defined in natural law."[38] Moreover, Niebuhr is quite emphatic that the classical rationalism of natural law theory in the church does not understand history. Roman Catholic appeals to natural law "therefore do not understand the uniqueness of historical occasions or the historical biases which creep into the definitions of natural law. . . . How, for instance, can one declare property to be a right according to natural law when the institution of property represents such various types of power and responsibility in various historical settings?"[39] This observation does not, of course, mean that Niebuhr rejects the idea of abiding principles of justice. Justice, however, is an application of the law of love.

From this comment by Niebuhr it must not be inferred that the Roman Catholic writers do not take account of the contingencies of varying circumstances. Niebuhr, Brunner, Ramsey, and Knudson, for example, are all aware that allowances are made for particular situations. But Ramsey's criticism of Maritain points out the special difficulty involved in his attempt to have the *jus gentium,* or the relative natural law operating under special circumstances, follow from first principles in a necessary manner. "How can a natural law without definite content follow in such necessary fashion simply from reflecting on man as man or for that matter from anything? And how can anything else follow in such necessary fashion from a natural law which itself has no specific content, even supposing any number of conditions of fact?" Ramsey suggests that either the natural law has content or else "by natural law is meant only a form of intuition ethics, possibly quite variable intuitions."[40]

8. In Aquinas' ethic the distinction between an absolute and a relative natural law became involved in the sharp distinction between nature and super-nature. Both the relative and absolute natural law, he held, belonged to nature. Above nature was the realm of grace and the sphere of Christian perfection. This involved the whole ethic in a false though often ambiguous dualism. The reason was that the natural law was held to participate in eternal law and was harmonious therefore with grace, while at the same time it was also a vehicle of compromise with the predicaments of social life. As a result, for example, the New Testament "communism" of love gave way to a justification of private property with appropriate moral checks, and the pacifism of the Sermon on the Mount gave way to a careful definition of a just war.[41] The relative natural law became, then, says Knudson, only a regulative ideal.

E. EVALUATIONS OF NATURAL LAW IN CONTEMPORARY PROTESTANT THEOLOGY

While critical of Roman Catholic treatments of natural law, many Protestant thinkers have not been able to dispense entirely with some basic elements in the idea. For example, Reinhold Niebuhr's strictures are significant, and yet we must note here his inability or unwillingness to dispose of natural law entirely. Even in his doctrine of love there are natural law elements. In *Faith and History* he argued that there were fewer specific principles of justice with "eternal" validity than is assumed in almost all theories of natural law. Moreover, rules of justice do not follow in a "necessary manner" from some basic proposition of justice. On the contrary, they are the fruit of a rational survey of the whole field of human interests, of the structure of human life and causal consequences in human relations.[42] This position is at this point quite similar to that of Roscoe Pound on precepts in the legal order and their relation to justice. Pound notes: " . . . we may say that some are just . . . at least in the sense of serving the purpose of the legal order . . . on the basis of reason, some only on the basis of experience that they have served that purpose well and long, and some on the basis of reason tested by experience or of experience developed by reason."[43] Niebuhr's thought, says John Bennett, "often seems to reject natural law altogether, but he draws back from the conclusion and presents at times a critical conception of natural law or a real Protestant substitute for natural law."[44] In commenting on Brunner, Niebuhr notes that Brunner tends increasingly to adopt, while he himself increasingly has rejected, the concept of natural law.[45] He goes too far when he says that in *Justice and the Social Order* Brunner reverts to an almost pure Thomism in seeking after a "justice which transcends human caprice and convention."

On the other hand he criticizes Karl Barth's work *Christengemeinde und Bürgergemeinde* for being unnecessarily cryptic and embarrassed about the fact that there are implied standards of natural law in his discussion of the justice of a state. The point that is involved here is Barth's initial rejection of natural law in his theological ethics because of his christological loyalty and his pessimistic view of human nature. Niebuhr rightly points out that for Barth the standards of justice in any society are so corrupted by sin that "only a mysterious overruling providence achieves the kind of social harmony and peace which are known in some states." On the contrary there is nothing so mysterious about the justice of healthy human communities; for, as Niebuhr sees it, this situation is a "revelation of man's residual capacity for justice, despite the corruptions of self-interest in his standards and in his practices."[46] This residual capacity refers of course to basic human nature.

Robert Fitch finds in Niebuhr a fourfold basis for a critical but affirmative reconstruction of the doctrine of a natural moral law while also providing a criticism of Niebuhr's point of view:

(1) The valuable insights and principles which Niebuhr allegedly has from beyond history are quite plainly to be found in history. The Christian revelation, whatever its origin, occurred in history, is connected with precedent and subsequent history, and functions as a power in history. History is not as barren of structure and meaning as is supposed.

(2) Niebuhr's use of prophetic judgment in history appeals to a moral law of judgment in history.

(3) His doctrine of love has empirical bearings which must not be overlooked, for while it is not a "norm of history" it is yet a "primary law" of man's nature.

(4) His whole view may add up to some pattern of coherence in which polarities, dialectics, and ironies serve an affirmative function. Niebuhr has himself acknowledged these points in responding to Fitch.[47]

What needs to be brought out explicitly is that Niebuhr makes of the doctrine of love a new natural law while seeking to retain its translegal character. It is the source of the principle of equality.[48] Niebuhr recognizes that love must include freedom, order, and justice within its scope and application, but he recognizes also that these are not distinctively Christian principles. They are forced upon us by reflection upon the conditions of life. Love cannot repeal them, and love cannot work apart from them. Love obligates us in each situation to find the best pattern for the ordering of society in terms of these principles.[49] *Agape* is the negation and the fulfillment of all structures of justice. It is the source and end of all reciprocal relations in human existence, but it contradicts all schemes of justice insofar as they embody sinful elements. All genuine obedience to law is derived from the grace of love, which is more than law. Yet love is the final law of life. The *agape* of Christ is not arbitrarily imposed upon life. "It is 'from the beginning'; that is, it is given in the essential and created nature of man, which involves a freedom for which love is the only law."[50]

Niebuhr seems to arrive at a conception of love which is permeated by the rational demand for coherence and relevance. This is a very significant conception. It must be admitted, he says, "that the elaboration of the meaning of the Christian revelation demanded from the beginning, that the truth about life and God apprehended in an historical revelation be brought into final conformity with the truth which may be known by analyzing the structures and essences of reality on all levels."[51] In criticism of Niebuhr it must be said that the unity of reason and love is found only in personalistic terms in which faith is also an active venture. Reason of itself cannot compel faith or love, but there is a coherence in which love is the ultimate principle. This coherence is personal. The person is the concrete universal in whom the empirical coherence of reason, faith, and love is found.

A sharper contrast between love and natural law is found in the thought of Paul Ramsey. The natural law, if there be such, cannot be primary for Christians.[52] It was not decisive for Paul and therefore, by Ramsey's method of argumentation, it is not decisive. Since ethical orientation must focus in Christ, it is not a principle which conforms to man's natural conscience. "Christian ethics is an ethics of perfection which cuts man to fit the pattern, not the pattern to fit man: how then can any major part of its fundamental content be drawn from man?"[53] Jesus Christ is the one and only teacher of Christians. We have already noted Ramsey's specific criticisms of the natural law as defined by Maritain. Here we need only note his rejection of all "coalition ethics,"[54] i.e., of all ethics which seek to unite philosophical and theological standpoints. His standpoint is that of Christ *transforming* natural law.[55] He concedes that "the rights of men" have validity apart from the Christian understanding of being in the image of God, but he transforms the essential historical meaning of right. The motivation for valuing human personality he derives neither from the created nature of man nor indirectly by implication from man's created capacity for responsive service to God, but centrally from within the service itself.[56] "No moral judgment," says Ramsey, "is sufficient by nature alone, without in one way or another the saving and transforming power of the *agape* of Christ."[57]

Emil Brunner, we noted at the opening of this chapter, appreciates the fundamental intention of the natural law of justice but finds the use of the term so confused today that he thinks it better to abandon it altogether.[58] Nevertheless, his idea of the Christian conception of justice is very close to the classical norm. What corresponds to the Creator's ordinance is just, and the ordinance bestows on every creature, with its being, the law of its being and its relationship to other creatures. "The rights of man are rights which, so to speak, God gives men at their birth. The rights of communities are rights which go back to a definite relationship between men based on the order of creation. . . . In the last resort all justice means these constants of creation as a basis on which every human being receives his due."[59] Sidney Cave brings the English tradition in ethics into an approval of Brunner. Though the Christian derives his knowledge of the good not from the surmises of his "practical reason" but from the revelation of God in Jesus, nevertheless there is in all men some power to know the good. The concept of the natural law expresses the basic principle of justice and provides the basis of co-operation between Christians and non-Christians. The peace of the world depends on this, says Cave.[60]

Joseph Fletcher, whose criticisms of Roman Catholic interpretations of natural law we have noted, also recommends abandoning the term "natural law" because of the perversions to which it has been subjected. Perhaps the term "moral order" is better. Certainly ethical realism must be acknowledged. There is a moral order, objectively existent, to which both individuals and the law of the community are subordinate. Morality is a part of reality. We seek it but we do not make it. "Medieval and ancient moralists called it the Natural Law; religionists call it the Will of God; our American founding fathers, in the Declaration of Independence, called it 'certain unalienable rights.' Whatever name we give it, it is there. Morality is an aspect of what is, as well as an ideal of what ought to be."[61] Such an ethical realism is an article of faith, but not for that reason irrational. We have to be ethical relativists as far as the content of knowledge is concerned. Ethical values are always subject to correction by fresh experiences and capable of greater depth and scope as science, technology, and social progress increase our insights and add to the power of control over self and the external world.

Archbishop Temple was an ethical realist who stressed the need for rational order and balance in Christian living and presented the objective structure of law as the right basis for ordering society. He kept in balance the views that values are objective, that natural ends are to be realized in fellowship, and that the Christian ethic of love is not in conflict with justice but that justice is the first stage of the complete expression of love.[62] But while the principle of justice comes first, Temple held it must contribute to the whole conception of the purpose of human life in the Christian view. One must begin with this whole conception of ends. "Man is created for fellowship in the family of God: fellowship first with God, and through that with all God's other children."[63] That is the primary test that must be applied to every social system. Hence, for example, the real defense of democracy is this: people called upon to exercise responsible judgment on the matters before the country develop their own personal qualities by so doing. He said, referring to the people, "You make them feel that they belong to one another in this corporate society, and so you deepen and intensify personal fellowship." The Christian message gives full content and understanding to personal relationships through fellowship.

In opposition to the types of Protestant thought thus far presented is a theologian like N. H. Søe, who opposes Christocracy to all forms of the natural law. He vigorously criticizes Brunner's effort to begin with the Aristotelian concept of justice. Ethical goals, moreover, do not belong to the domain of the intellect. Conflicts of goals are issues of one faith versus another, and in this the only Christian standpoint can be: "Jesus Christ is Lord." Love is ultimate; but one must not, like Luther, put it into the spiritual realm alone. Luther too narrowly restricted love and he was wrong in making it a kind of law of nature in the spiritual realm, thus imprisoning it there. The standpoint of Christocracy is inclusive. Søe rejects the view which he ascribes to William Temple that the theologian preaches the Word to the statesman who then uses technical means responsibly. On the contrary, the church indicates to the statesman the will of God in concrete cases. Here Søe supports Karl Barth. The theologian must in his capacity as theologian take a stand on a concrete issue as, for example, on the remilitarization of Germany. He must know the arguments on both sides, the facts, and the issues. Then as theologian he must give more than a relative judgment; he must give a Christian witness. The state must serve Christ, who is Lord of all. There is no basis for the state in a justice which is not derived from the Christian doctrine of love.[64]

Søe, who follows Karl Barth closely but not slavishly, recognizes, of course, that Christianity enters into a world which is already furnished with some fixed structures. Social life before the proclamation of the gospel must have some kind of moral rules; hence some ethics is independent of Christian revelation. And Christian teaching does not completely change or abolish these structures and ethics. Christians ought to be happy when they find more or less deep-going agreement with their non-Christian fellowmen on ethical issues. Co-operation as far as possible is an obvious Christian obligation. The Christian idea of humanity and of natural love is based on the idea that Christ died for us all. Christians do not know any "special" Christ, for the world was created in him and to him. Søe does not object to the phrase used by H. H. Schrey of a "Christological Natural Law."[65]

F. A PERSONALISTIC VIEW OF NATURAL LAW

How shall we resolve the basic issue of whether there is a natural moral law and how it may be known? The system of moral laws climaxing in the personalistic and communitarian laws points the way for the answers to these questions. There is moral law and it can be known. In addition to the formulation of moral law it is important to indicate how the moral laws relate to metaphysical issues; for the natural law theory has in its classical formulation related the norms of justice to the nature and will of God. One modern theorist concludes that the point where values and norms coincide, which is the ultimate origin of law and at the same time the beginning of the moral life proper, is what the natural law means.[66]

The relation of religion and ethics has generally been quite close. When religion is defined as co-operation between man and God expressed through worship and conduct of life, God is viewed as the embodiment of the moral ideal and as the source or creator of a moral order in the universe.[67] True value, on this basis, is seen to be theogenetic. In a sense, however, ethics is logically more ultimate than religion, though not logically or metaphysically more ultimate than God, inasmuch as it is impossible to regard any being as good unless one has some conception of what "good" is.[68] Even "revealed" good is judged or claimed to be so by some human agent. It would be unreasonable to believe in the existence of a good God unless experience offered evidence of goodness. Ideas of God and man on the moral side are, when consistently developed, polar conceptions. "Ethics is, therefore, logically prior to religion; religion cannot be true unless ethics is true, but ethics might be true and religion false."[69] This view would seem to oppose those foregoing discussions of natural law in which theologians have consistently held that the Christian ethic is morally superior to all natural law.

The great advances of religion have generally been evidenced by the moral critique of prevailing religious standards and practices. But morality is not entirely independent of religion. Morality is dependent on religion for some of its content. The whole course of Western civilization has been a confluence of biblical and nonbiblical traditions. "Morality," says Brightman, "does not derive the Law of the Most Inclusive End . . . from religious faith, but if that Law be true and if religion be a real value, then it is a part of one's duty to worship God and (in accordance with the Law of the Best Possible) to achieve the highest type of religion of which one is capable."[70] The moral law therefore requires a serious consideration of the religious life including, of course, the Christian faith. The moralist should take from the Christian faith its profoundest ethical values and organize them coherently into personal and community existence when these values are criticized and interpreted. The actual Christian community is not always clear as to what coherent Christian values are.

Not only does ethics get from religion some of its content but it recognizes that if the existence of God be a reality, then he is

the creator of persons as moral beings and therefore, in this sense,
autonomy depends on theonomy.[71] Brightman and Tillich are together in this conception. Brightman defines theonomy as "the
belief that the basic laws of the universe (the laws of the physical
universe and of ideal values alike) are laws of the will of God and
constitute the conditions of all possible and valuable achievement."[72] Tillich defines theonomy as asserting "that the superior
law is, at the same time, the innermost law of man himself, rooted
in the divine ground which is man's own ground: the law of life
transcends man, although it is, at the same time his own."[73] Such
a view of theonomy does not contradict the moral law of autonomy but gives it a metaphysical context. Thus this moral law
is no arbitrary creation of the will of God, but rather an expression
of the *reason* of God, which is eternal and uncreated.[74] It should be
noted that though Brightman and Tillich hold similar positions on
theonomy the latter holds to an ontology which ultimately places
being above personality, whereas Brightman's view is thoroughly
personalistic. "God's authority is an authority that not only recognizes, but even creates, freedom," he says. For Brightman autonomy is the guide to theonomy and embodies the truth in the
scholastic view of the law of nature and the eternal law while rejecting its ontology. The concrete ethical and religious idea for
Tillich is a "theonomous culture," by which he means one whose
expressions are creations of an "ultimate concern and a transcending meaning not as something strange but as its own spiritual
ground." The theonomous ethic for Brightman means a personalistic divine-human community in which the finite persons are
dependent on the Supreme Person, but are free and mutually
transcend each other. *Logos* and *agape* characterize the mind and
will of God, who seeks to achieve in the created society along
with himself a barrierless community of realized persons. Religion and ethics are united through faith in a free commitment to
God in which service to him means also the highest interpersonal
realization of men.

In this emphasis on theonomy the theory of moral law is close
to the view of Tillich, but recalls also Lehmann, Barth, and others
who are concerned about the will of God in action in his world.

Man's evaluations, choices, and decisions take place in a world which God in love has created. God sustains and brings to maturity all men, including the rebellious ones who deny his existence. Thus theonomy transcends the church, while it includes it, and recognizes that in Christ, the cosmic Son of the eternal Father, all men are created and loved. Since the universe is a divine and personal society, each moral situation is one in which the finite persons confront afresh their divinely personal ground. The reality of the moral laws in no way detracts from the responsive character of each personal existential occasion calling for ethical decision. Indeed, it closes a gap in Christian social ethics and invites its development as an interdisciplinary field of study.

IX

JESUS CHRIST
AND RESPONSIBLE COMMUNITY

If the Christian faith is ultimately true, it is because the claims about Jesus Christ as central to ethical adequacy are coherent with all the relevant evidence. The present chapter is an interpretation of Jesus Christ and his relationship to responsible community. As here presented the interpretation shows the impact of ecumenical discussions in recent decades and personal reflection on the moral laws. On the one hand, there are also affinities to Christian ethical expositions such as by Lehmann, Fletcher, De-Wolf, and Ramsey. On the other hand, this expression of faith in Jesus Christ shows the need for the kinds of moral law formulations as have been made in Chapter III and developed in Chapters IV, V, VI, and VII. The New Testament's relation to responsible present-day moral valuation and decision is penetrating, pervasive, and transforming, and yet it is indirect in the sense that no moral judgments in concrete cases ought to be direct deductions from biblical statements.

A. COHERENCE AND CHRISTIAN ETHICS

The kinds of choices that persons ought to make should be coherent with the best scientific understanding and empirical knowledge, with theoretical reflection on moral principles and methods, and with the highest acts of faith in divine self-disclosure. Christian ethicists who reject moral philosophy would agree with the present interpretation at least in distinguishing binding Christian relationships and demands from legalistic prescriptions drawn from or deduced from Scripture. There would be a common concern also for coherence, but there is a major difference in how coherence is interpreted.

Barth, Ramsey, and Lehmann demand that Christian ethics be coherent with Jesus Christ. The position in this book is that as an interdisciplinary field Christian social ethics should be coherent scientifically, philosophically, and theologically, no one discipline dictating the coherence. This issue is, of course, basic. According to Karl Barth the theologian relates himself to ethics as reflection in several ways: (1) he will proceed from God's relation to man and only then continue with man's relation to God; (2) he starts steadily and happily with the Bible; (3) he does not deny, nor is he ashamed of, his indebtedness to a particular philosophy or ontology, to ways of thought and speech; yet he stands ready to submit the coherence of his concepts and formulations to the coherence of the divine revelation and *not conversely;* (4) he thinks and speaks within the church, within the communion of saints, loving positive tasks in and through the Christian community; and (5) he works in *communication* with other theologians and grants them the same freedom with which he is entrusted.[1]

There is much that is appealing in Barth's position as here outlined. Yet on the crucial limitation given to coherence it must be rejected in favor of empirical open-ended coherence. To be sure truth should correspond to ultimate reality and knowledge should cohere with truth. Man's experiences should cohere with God; man is not the criterion of God. Obviously! Objective reality within man or outside him should control his ideas and provide the referents of his trust and faith. But, when revelation means what is interpreted in and about the Bible, the criterion is constantly altered. The appeal that ethical reflection must cohere with divine revelation does not recognize sufficiently the changing traditions about that self-disclosure, the historical and cultural factors in these changing interpretations, and the part that science and philosophy inevitably play in Christian faith and understanding. There is no completed given event with which ethical reflection can cohere—against all other evidence. It is the ethical reflection which must be coherent with all the relevant evidence. This coherence is not somehow given to man but must be found continually as an emergent.

A radical personalistic interpretation is in order at this point. Barth and Bonhoeffer are probably right in calling for the acknowledgment of God as eternally acting. He is eternally energizing. Bowne, Brightman, and DeWolf would agree that to be is to act and to act is to will. God acts. Man is God's creature. Man acts within the context of God's acting. God is for man, though he is also in whatever way he chooses for himself—but these ways are consistent. God is transcendent and immanent. Man is created for himself, for fellowman, and for God. He is to a degree self-transcendent. Man is a being who knows and acts through transactions. These transactions are active events; some are conscious; some are subconscious. He acts, interacts, responds, and the like. His privacy is his own. To be fully known he must, in this sense like God, disclose himself. He discloses himself and makes claims.

Man's reflective theories about Christian ethics—like his knowledge about nature and social groups—get their data from interaction and response. If it is true that "we love because God first loved us," it is true that man gets his data from what in his experience God has already done. Since God keeps on acting and disclosing himself through energizing events, man cannot predict with certainty about the future because all predictions are at best based on what God has already done. Cognitively speaking man deals in probabilities based on the record of God's acting up to now. Man is a predicter who never catches the Ultimate in the act of initiating. Man's ideas, intentions, trust, faith, and deeds enter a stream of events whose ground is ultimately dynamic on terms other than his own—except as God calls him to co-creation, co-redemption, co-service, and the like.

The limitations of knowledge and of faith are both functions of man's creaturehood. These do not entitle him to skepticism or to relativism but they indicate why any coherence must always be open-ended. Theological tradition, for example, grows not only because we know more about what happened in and to Jesus in the first century, but because the God who acted in Jesus keeps acting—and does so literally all over the place.

Man's response to God should be full and complete, and for

this reason, if for no other, the coherence of his ethical reflections should be interdisciplinary. The coherence must therefore be empirical and open-ended or emergent. We should work in the faith of Christian experience that whenever *agape* in Christ is related to open-minded philosophical ethics and the work of behavioral sciences, the personal power of Jesus will be manifest. Faith and reason are not conflicting principles. They interpenetrate in man's spiritual unity.

B. JESUS CHRIST AS CENTRAL

Jesus Christ, or the Christ-event, has generally been focal in theological ethics. A sharply focused christological ethics has dominated recent literature. In ecumenical circles this emphasis has been further encouraged by world-wide study programs specializing on Christ's relation to his church. While this significant quest for the basic unity of the Christian community continues, corrective protests are also being made. Some protest a Christology which may not do justice to the full idea of the Trinity, particularly to the doctrines of creation and the work of the Holy Spirit. An adequately grounded theological ethic must be related to God as Creator and Preserver and to the Holy Spirit as present in the church and the world as well as to the person of Jesus Christ and to God as Redeemer. In Christology it is essential to emphasize both the cosmic Christ, i.e., the love and power of God revealed in Christ, and the historically powerful Jesus Christ who is thoroughly rooted in the whole human community and especially in the Old Testament community. In Judaism and in Jesus' life and teaching, love of God and love of neighbor are integrally united. The life, the teaching, and the revelation of God in Jesus Christ point to the widest contexts of God's work in creation and redemption and express the need for and the practical possibility of man's response to God's love. This response gives rise to responsible community. Thus while rejecting a christomonistic focus, theological ethics must recognize Jesus' central significance.

Jesus stressed the wholeness of morality. He emphasized the personal dispositions of the will and the other personal qualities which have ethical significance. He emphasized also the Kingdom of God, God's righteous rule, and man's relations to his neighbor. Goodness is, therefore, to be manifested in every phase of the moral life within, including motives, disposition, and character, and in the deeds which express these outwardly in social relationships.

C. JESUS CHRIST AS GROUND, GOAL, AND MOTIVE OF RESPONSIBLE COMMUNITY

In what sense may Jesus Christ be spoken of as the ground of responsible community? He is the revelation of God's redemptive activity with respect to his creation. The disciples of Jesus are linked to him not only through a personal loyalty but also through a new covenant which relates the mighty acts of God in pre-Christian history to the great purpose of bringing to pass a barrierless community of righteousness and love. Christians pray, "Thy will be done, on earth as it is in heaven"! Jesus is the one who points to God's spiritual covenant with men. He grounds the responsible society in his life, teaching, work, death, and resurrection taken as a total revelatory event. This inclusive revelation bears witness to the power and love of God. Henceforth God is revealed as Christlike, so that the Creator and Law-Giver is also known as Redeemer.

The creative power of God is also loving and redeeming activity. All things are made through him and by him who is loving creativity. Thus the idea of the responsible society, as developed in ecumenical circles, is grounded in the character of God as revealed in Christ. The term "Christ" here emphasizes the loving personal Lordship of the divine will expressed in the forgiveness of sins. Aspects of the Lordship and redemptive activity of God are expressed in such concepts as the law of love, the law of righteousness, and the Kingdom of God.

Jesus Christ is the ground for responsible community through his words of ethical authority. Jesus' own authority was, in human terms, charismatic. Yet the ethical appeal of Jesus is central in his preaching and teaching. His words have tremendous moral power. The Sermon on the Mount lays on all an ultimate and immediate demand. It emerges in an imperative of perfection whose ultimate authority is the ethical purity and holiness of God. Whatever and whomever God includes in his sphere of responsible concern is the object also of man's ethical involvement.

Christians believe that ultimate power belongs to God, and therefore in the most trying social and historical circumstances they may trust in his help. Faith in Christ means a reliance on God's righteousness and mercy, for in Christ his followers are involved in sharing the world's problems and in being aware of their solidarity with all human beings. When Christians ground their ethics in Jesus Christ, they appeal not only to the goodness of Jesus' personal life but to the cosmic Christ, i.e., to God in whom creative power and righteous love are indivisibly one. This ethical love sustains responsive community.

The cosmic ground is historically active. In Jesus Christ divine love is manifested in concrete historical form. He is the revelation of cosmic foundations for righteous community living, and he is also the ground of the responsible society through his historical existence. He is personal power in human history. Some contemporary Christian ethical theory focuses on love primarily as a norm which transcends history. But such a view leaves out of account a most crucial consideration. Responsibility to God for the neighbor was in Jesus not only lifted up as a norm; it was manifested in history in his person. Moreover, it functions as ongoing moral power incarnate in culture. In the early church the community ethic was a continuation of love in the sense of *agape*.

Jesus manifested the incarnate concern of God for all earthly tasks and the duty to take up the burdens of daily life. Hence attention must be directed to the wholeness of the person of Jesus to correct the tendency to abstract certain traits of his character and work and to deal with these as concepts or principles in isolation from a synoptic view of his personality. His attitudes expressed toward wealth, rulers, sickness, the poor, children, and the like, as well as toward suffering, persecution, compassion, and piety, are often isolated by theologians from the unity of his personal existence. Personality explains the various ethical principles, concepts, and values and is always more and deeper than the systematized sum of them. The saving power of Jesus is the whole response he calls forth. His historical actuality is the ultimate attestation of the relevance of his love to all social situations.

Jesus Christ is the goal as well as the ground of responsible society. In what sense is this the case? Persons are the subjects of moral responsibility and the ends for which society exists. Jesus Christ is the historical manifestation of the fulfillment of creation in a completely obedient Son. Human nature is actualized in self-giving love. In the freely accepted and adequate obedience of Jesus, God has shown the kind of person who is the goal of history. Jesus is the personal norm of all social goals.

The Christian ethic has an imperative form, but it is none the less teleological. Obedience to God's will is integrally united in Jesus to perfectionist goals. The historical community and the individual person have vocations in God's purposive creation. In the biblical perspective the vocation of man is both in history and beyond history. The true end of society is not the mere pursuit of abstract ends under ideal norms, but the realization of personal trust in God and fulfillment in community. The biblical inspiration for this is amply illustrated in several passages: "But seek first his kingdom and his righteousness . . ." (Matt. 6:33); "You, therefore, must be perfect, as your heavenly Father is perfect" (Matt. 5:48). The writer of the Letter to the Ephesians includes most of these motifs within a cosmic perspective: "He destined us in love to be his sons through Jesus Christ, according to the purpose of his will, to the praise of his glorious grace which he freely bestowed on us in the Beloved" (Eph. 1:5-6). The teleological, the imperative, and the indicative accents of the biblical ethic are combined in such a verse as the following: "Therefore be imitators of God, as beloved children. And walk in love, as Christ loved us and gave himself up for us . . ." (Eph. 5:1-2).

The purposive perfectionism of Jesus' ethic is found in the Lord's Prayer, "Thy kingdom come, thy will be done, on earth as it is in heaven" (Matt. 6:10). The ethical urgency of the commands of righteousness and love is not primarily determined by the calendar but by the imperatives of the divine will. The sense of urgency is deepened as men have moved away from speculation and calculation of possible future events to an awareness of the absolute goodness of God as revealed in Jesus and expressed in the idea of the cosmic Christ of later theology. The norm of perfection is God. In the great eschatological parable of the last judgment (Matt. 25:31-46) the urgency of the Kingdom is closely tied to the vocation of service to the needy through whom God calls.

The Christian hope looks toward the future through the normative eyes of Jesus Christ and sees at the end (both as *telos* and *finis*) the consummation of God's work. Like the early Christians, present-day Christians (and with them all men) live under the judgment of God and under the promise of his forgiving love. His is the Kingdom and the power and the glory. All times are times of his creative, righteous, and redeeming love. His active personal relationship to man and to society is referred to in the Bible as his coming. The early church recognized the fact that God had come to men in a special way through Jesus. A new era had been inaugurated in human history through his coming and through the establishment of his church. Jesus Christ was more than a norm. He had conquered sin and death. That which God had disclosed and shared with men through Christ was an initial and decisive victory for mankind over evils and fears which had blocked the life of faith and trust. Even the defeat of the cross had been overcome by God in raising Jesus from the dead. The redemptive purpose of God made manifest in this way would in his own time be brought to its complete fulfillment. God had taken the loving initiative in man's salvation and he would finish the work he had begun, for it is through his loving will that the whole creation had come into being.

The goal of God's mighty acts includes not only the future but links this goal to the past and the present. The reality and the power of his Kingdom are not yet fully revealed, but we live in a world which is his creation and in a history whose meaning has been disclosed in the life and work of Jesus. "God so loves his world that he gave his only son for man's salvation. His providence governs it, and his spirit lives and works in the midst of it, overcoming evil with good in countless ways, and bringing to fruit beyond human expectation of contrivance the deeds of devoted men and women. But neither the world of nature nor the world of men is as yet what God would have it be. Both are still enmeshed in the disorder of the unredeemed age and await their liberation."[2]

As Jesus Christ is not only the ground and the goal of responsible community, he is also the motive for its realization. In what
sense is Jesus the motive? The love of God in Christ calls out
man's responding love. "We love, because he first loved us"
(1 John 4:19). It is not simply that the good is worthy to be
chosen. Perfection motivates. Beyond the motivation of ideal
ends, Jesus helps men to have faith that God accepts them. This
faith is itself not dependent on any previous condition of moral
excellence or obedience. In relating men to God's saving forgiveness, Jesus arouses faith in God as merciful Father. Through
faith men are reborn, and their self-centered and anxious selves
are reconstituted. Self-will is thereafter subordinated to the love
of God and love of neighbor. The self becomes grateful to God
and desires more fully to do his will. Man becomes a servant to
meet human need. He serves his neighbor like Christ.

The motives of responsible society, then, are not only aspirations for perfection, desires for righteousness, and hopes for the
future. Deepest of all is the freely accepted love of God which
reaches out to others. The love of neighbor is in Jesus a universal
idea. Man as man is the object of love. Just as faith in God is pre-
determined by no previous moral excellence, so the community of
loving concern is a barrierless community. This makes the whole
world the object of Christian ethics and all mankind the scope of
the moral situation in which the specific duties are then defined.

The love of God in Jesus is not only a memory recorded in the
Scriptures and not only a goal to which one aspires; it is a present
relationship which sustains and motivates. Loyalty to Jesus Christ
is personal. The love of God is a present power. Men may have
the assurance now of forgiveness and acceptance. Thus they
stand not only under the judgment of God but they live in the
present mercy of God's holy love. There is an imperative ethical
urgency but there is also forgiveness for moral failure. In this
relationship lives become fruitful in virtue and service. This relationship is morally free in the sense that men can fall away from
faith and be disloyal to their vocation as sons of God. Moral effort and decision are required to keep faith real and vital. The
grace of God is freely bestowed, but it is appropriated through
the moral effort of decisions involving faith.

Since free response characterizes man's highest encounter with that which is ultimate, i.e., with God, religious freedom is the most basic of liberties and the root of all other moral and social freedoms.

Not from outer compulsion or heteronomous commands but from inner springs of spiritual life the Christian responds to the call of God and neighbor. Deep calls to deep. Jesus said to the woman at the well, ". . . whoever drinks of the water that I shall give him will never thirst; the water that I shall give him will become in him a spring of water welling up to eternal life" (John 4:14). In the Sermon on the Mount the inner qualities of right action are expounded in the Beatitudes: humility, meekness, hunger for righteousness, mercy, purity, and loyalty to the Kingdom of God. Other inner dispositions and virtues which are extolled are forgiveness, self-renunciation, going the "second mile," loving the unlovely, unostentatious worship, trust in God, compassion, and striving for perfection. The most personal faith motivates the freest universal responsibility.

D. JESUS CHRIST,
THE LORD OF THE WORLD
AND THE CHURCH

Christianity's greatest contribution to the religious and moral life of the world is not some lofty ethical principles but its gospel of Jesus Christ. Its central contribution is an actual personality, full, mature, concrete. The church has asserted and is now asserting that he is Lord of the world and the church. What does this mean? In what sense is this true? Christians affirm that if he is not Lord of all he is not Lord at all. This assertion involves the task of understanding what Christ's Lordship means as an ecumenical witness under present-day conditions and in the concrete situations in which Christians and non-Christians find themselves together.

The term "Lord" may be taken in so transcendent and austere a sense that Jesus Christ is interpreted primarily as Judge. Through many centuries of the Christian church this view tended to be dominant. Some recent theological thought has reinforced the idea of the divine righteousness in such a way as to cast a pessimistic shadow over the church and the world and to make this shadow so dark that the relevance of Jesus Christ for personal and social redemption has been made obscure. What, contrariwise, should be affirmed is that he who is sovereign Lord is also Redeemer, a present living power in the life of the individual believer, in the fellowship of the believers, and in the social order. In thinking of Christ's Lordship one must make a distinction but not a separation between Jesus' historical authority and God's acts as Creator, Redeemer, and Holy Spirit. The Lordship of Christ refers not only to past events but to God's present actions and to his claims on future historical events. Redemption in the church and redemption of the world, though not now fully accomplished, are implied in the idea of Christ's Lordship. Such faith and hope go beyond the idea, so frequently expressed, that men may be saved in principle but not in fact. Here is the crucial issue of much contemporary Christian ethics. It is closely related to the question of how the church and world are related under the Lordship of Christ.

Daniel D. Williams illuminates this issue when he says: "The problem is to understand the relation between two aspects of our actual history: the ongoing of human events with all their mixture of good and evil, and the history of God's redemptive activity culminating in Christ and continuing in his Church. . . . The Bible sees these two histories as finally one; for there is one God and one creation, and real history is simply the story of God's dealing with his creation."[3] This is the constructive perspective from which to perceive the relation of Christ's authority both to the secular order and to the church, both in his relation to ultimate norms of moral judgment and to concrete historical involvement.

This formulation by Williams is supported also in the later writings of Barth which stress the "humanity of God" and note the inclusive community of Christians and non-Christians, the so-called outsiders in relation to so-called insiders. ". . . Thinking in terms of the humanity of God, we cannot at all reckon in a serious way with *real* 'outsiders,' with a 'world come of age,' but only with a world which *regards* itself as of age (and proves daily that it is precisely not that). Thus the so-called 'outsiders' are really only 'insiders' who have not yet understood and apprehended themselves as such. On the other hand, even the most persuaded Christian, in the final analysis, must and will recognize himself ever and again as an 'outsider.' So there must then be no particular language for insiders and outsiders. Both are contemporary men-of-the-world—all of us are."[4] In some Roman Catholic theology the term "People of God" today denotes the element of divine life in history, God's total life in mankind. This expresses a very broad context. Some use this term "People of God" for the church as a way to denote mankind insofar as it is now consecrated to God, because of the fact of Christ, and in a situation of salvation objectively possible for every man.[5]

It is theologically evident that no human society, either in so-called Christian or in non-Christian countries, is obedient to Christ's way or fully related to him in any strict or even adequate degree. It is also evident that the church as a community is, like the world, under the judgment of God. No part of the visible church and no member of the church has fully done what is morally and religiously required. In the light of the ideal and of the ultimate norm all stand condemned. In these two senses, then, it would appear that Christ is not Lord of the world or of the church. It may indeed be asked: If men are not fully obedient to Christ, how then is he Lord?

Some take the view that in Jesus Christ God has already won the victory over all the powers of evil in principle and that all which remains is to manifest this fully in glory when his time will have come. Using the figure of warfare they allege that the decisive battle has taken place (in the life, death, and resurrection of Jesus), the power of the enemy is broken, and nothing remains but "mopping up" operations.

Figures of speech are always dangerous and never more so than in dealing with ultimate questions. The above figure may tend to obscure several crucial points: (1) that God's relation to man is of a moral and spiritual order and therefore man's response cannot be coerced. The future must always, therefore, be a fresh victory for the forces of redemption. Though cosmic and historical resources are available, they must constantly be sought after in new struggles with evil. The God of Jesus Christ is Lord of uncoerced man in the sense that only through free obedience can man achieve the fulfillment of life for which he was created. Man revolts against his own deepest nature—his own highest good—when he revolts against the ethical love of God. Yet God continues to command, and he alone is worthy to receive man's ultimate loyalty, for man is God's creature.

(2) The cosmic Christ is the highest good of all men, not just of men in the church. He transforms the values already achieved in the various cultures of mankind by purging them and bringing them into full realization.

(3) No other lordship will ultimately prevail. Provisional expressions of justice and love are all made possible in that they are dependent on the one ultimate source of good. All true values are ultimately theogenetic wherever they are realized or experienced in the world. Knowingly or unknowingly they are dependent on the cosmic Christ, God in his redemptive and loving creativity. All forms of human good finally testify to the sustaining love and power of God. All human forms of good are judged by ultimate good.

(4) Jesus Christ as historical incarnation of God is not operationally Lord in any strict temporal sense of having actual effective power over all that happens in the church or in the world outside it. But he is Lord in the sense that he was and is the bearer of the meaning of history. He is the concrete embodiment of the cosmic personal norm of righteous love. The Kingdom of God was present in history in Jesus Christ and all the kingdoms of man must come to terms with the God who was incarnate in him. To the extent that he is acknowledged and obeyed, to that extent his operational Lordship is extended; yet many who acknowledge him do not fully obey him. To the world that does not know him or obey him Jesus Christ makes a claim and directs a mission.

(5) The Lordship of Christ over the church is in one sense like his Lordship over the world: he gives it meaning, life, and goal. Yet the visible churches often only disobediently acknowledge him as when their sins are manifest in failure to witness or in disunity. This is what it means to say that Christ and the Kingdom

of God judge the church. Christ has thus a positive and a negative, or dialectical, relation to the church as to the world. Their good is not possible except through him and yet they are morally in tension with his commands.

(6) But the Lordship of Christ over the church is distinguishable from his cosmic and historical Lordship over the world because of his presence in its fellowship as memory, living power, and abiding Holy Spirit. The church is a fellowship of the forgiven and forgiving, and thus he sustains a more direct saving relationship to her than to groups and persons who have not entered into the life of the church and taken upon themselves his work of unity, reconciliation, and mission to the world. He is the Lord who sets her to tasks of service and redemption and who defines her vocation, sustaining her by his presence and power. "The ethical reality of the church," says Paul Lehmann, "is the building up of itself in love, as Christ the head works in it; and this ethical reality is the *koinonia*."[6]

(7) He is finally also Lord over the world in that he intends responsible society. He has given as the goal the creation in history of a barrierless community for the whole of mankind. Each man has a vocation to serve to bring this community into existence. Hence neither Christ's cosmic ultimacy nor the historical reality of his power are grounds for an attitude of social passivity. On the one hand, Christians often fall into the temptation of waiting on God to take responsibility for them. To wait passively on heavenly interventions often means encouraging the worst of earthly corruptions. On the other hand, an enthusiastic activism which identifies the right response of the church uncritically with a particular power strategy or program also misjudges the nature of the tension between God and man.

E. JESUS CHRIST AND THE KINGDOM OF GOD

The idea of the Kingdom of God, so central to the teachings of Jesus in the Synoptic Gospels, repeats or overlaps much that we have already outlined. It is the most comprehensive concept which expresses the reign of God in the lives of men and societies. God's sovereign rule is at once an eternal fact, a present

manifestation and demand in the lives of men, and a consummation still to come.[7] To the first-century Jews to whom Jesus spoke
it was not a new theme. Nowhere in the Gospels does he define
the phrase, though he illuminates it in sayings and parables. Jesus
promised entrance to the Kingdom to an entirely different group
of people from those whom most had expected he would. He affirmed a preliminary realization of the sovereignty of God in his
own ministry. He took the Kingdom hope of his people with a
new seriousness. The righteous God of history was about to assert
his full sovereignty.[8]

Social responsibility before God is inherent in the idea of the
Kingdom. It is not limited to any previous historical people who
entertained the idea. On the contrary it is an inclusive idea
broader than the church but equally historical. It is as universal in
scope as the will of God for and in history.

Yet the idea of the Kingdom is linked to Jesus' own ministry as
well as to God's righteous reign. The Kingdom was manifest in
Jesus' life concretely, and at the same time he points beyond
himself to the full scope of its activity as God's sovereign will.
Christians who acknowledge loyalty to Jesus are led at once to the
attitude of social responsibility which he taught and embodied.
Men who begin Christian moral reflection with the concept of the
Kingdom of God are confronted with the claim that its meaning
was made manifest in Jesus. Jesus' own ministry is thus an in-
escapable aspect of the Kingdom concept. It is related, on the
one hand, to his life and teaching about God and, on the other
hand, to his death and resurrection. He is the central member and
event in that dimension of the Kingdom of God which has to do
with its earthly expression. Theologically speaking, we cannot define a responsible society anywhere in the world apart from the
Kingdom of God, and we cannot define the Kingdom apart from
Jesus' commanding personal relation to it. What we have said
above about Jesus Christ as ground, goal, and motive of the responsible society elaborates this theme. In an age of universal
history the center of meaning is God's love in Jesus Christ.

The idea of the Kingdom in relation to Jesus lifts up, once
again, concretely the social nature of man and the ideal of per-

sonality morally to be sought after. Is there a universal Christian style of life? Retrospectively considered, Christian history presents various ideal types like that of the desert anchorite, the feudal bishop-king, the crusader-knight, the catacomb slave, the monk, the poor priest, the reformer, the Puritan, the philanthropic capitalist, the circuit-rider, to mention only a few. None of these satisfies the full concrete universal of Christian personality. The transcendently ideal and the culturally immanent meet in dialectical tension in individual persons. Even in the case of the matchless personality of Jesus one must distinguish the genuinely universal from the historically particular. Jesus is not to be culturally imitated.

An adequate view of man requires a social interpretation of the person as well as an understanding of his individual dynamic depth and freedom. When Jesus made his covenant with the disciples, he related it to the Kingdom. To this day the sacrament of the Eucharist is both a profoundly private and a profoundly solidaristic relationship.

The ideal social possibility of the Kingdom of God is the full actualization of personal and group relationships in love. Brotherhood and neighborliness are biblical expressions of it. Jesus significantly related such service and mutuality to God's will when he applied a passage from Isaiah to himself: "The Spirit of the Lord is upon me, because he has anointed me to preach good news to the poor. He has sent me to proclaim release to the captives and recovering of sight to the blind, to set at liberty those who are oppressed, to proclaim the acceptable year of the Lord" (Luke 4:18-19; cf. Isa. 61:1-2). To the extent that Jesus embodied this Kingdom of God ideal he gave expression not only to God's transcendent power, not only to the role of his cultural and religious milieu, but to his own personal creativity and response in history as well.

This emphasis on personal concreteness corrects the tendencies to use the idea of the Kingdom of God as a protest which favors transcendence over immanence. It corrects by resolving the conflict as pressed, for example, by Reinhold Niebuhr. "The fact is that the Kingdom of God represents a final and absolute possibility

which is, in some respects, equally distant from all political programs because all of them involve elements of coercion and re-
sistance which are foreign to a commonwealth of pure brotherhood
and love."[9] Stated in this transcendently abstract form, the Kingdom tends to become irrelevant to discriminate historical judgments. Such irrelevance is not, of course, Niebuhr's intention (he
is noted for concrete discriminate analyses), but he defaults on
the transition from ultimate perspectives to responsible social decision. He holds the realm of norms and the historical situation
abstractly apart. He does not begin, continue, and end with persons under God acting in history. This failure to be fully personalistic results in a view of the transcendent kingdom which
separates Jesus Christ from his fellowmen and the kingdom from
the will (or moral law) of God in history. The Kingdom must be
understood concretely in terms not only of norms but of personal
deeds of justice and love.

F. JESUS CHRIST AND THE LAW OF LOVE

God is love. God loves the world he has made. Since his creation is a society of persons, love is the ultimate cohesive power of
social order. God's love is infinite and boundless. Not only is
human consciousness social, but the divine consciousness is social
also. It is eternally social, the ground of all sociality and mutuality.
The love of God is the source of all human love. Yet the self-love
and egoistic drives of human beings threaten, distort, and even
destroy the mutuality and cohesion of true community, which
must constantly be renewed by saving self-knowledge, fresh dedi-
cation to the neighbor, and reconciliation with God.

Love is sometimes viewed less as a relationship of grace and
more as a norm or law. The conflict between love as taught by
Jesus and Paul and self-absorption in egoistic impulses is frequently overstated in current theology, as when Reinhold Niebuhr says: "the absolutism and perfectionism of Jesus' love ethic
sets itself uncompromisingly not only against the natural self-
regarding impulses, but against the necessary precedent defenses
of the self, required because of the egoism of others."[10] There
appears to be no bridge between the law of love so sharply

posed against man's nature and the concrete fulfillment of man's responsibilities to the neighbor. Niebuhr takes a basically different approach to love in one of his later essays, an approach based more on personal wholeness. "The ideal of love is not superimposed upon human history by scriptural, or any other, authority. Human existence, when profoundly analyzed, yields the law of love as the final law of human freedom. Man's unique freedom, in which he rises indeterminately above his determinate existence, requires that his life be fulfilled not within himself but in others. It also requires that his realization of himself in others should not be pursued merely from his own standpoint. That is, he cannot regard others simply as tools and instruments of his self-realization."[11]

Niebuhr believes that while the ultimate goal of the spirit of love is fulfillment for the self, this cannot be the intended goal; because as soon as men intend their own good they have lost the freedom from self-interest which can enable them to enter the self-realized community. Niebuhr's love ethic appears here to be impaled on the horns of dilemma and paradox.

Love as taught by Jesus does not require this paradox. Man is commanded to love his neighbor as himself. Self-love is not evil; it is not selfishness. What is affirmed in the New Testament is both man's *intention* to love and the recognition of the role of self-interest within the context of the community under God so that judgment, forgiveness, and service are all concurrently present. By wrestling with self-regarding impulses and by surrender to God man can love the neighbor. This point is directly affirmed in the parable of the Good Samaritan and the conversation that includes it. There is one inclusive context of love, the divinely personal community of self-giving (not self-repudiating) *agape*.[12]

Love expresses itself in the family bond, in ultimate desires and aspirations, in service to others, in creating the good community, in compassion, forgiveness, and self-sacrifice. Since love is freely given, writers often contrast it with justice, which measures to each what is his due and which supposedly can be coercively commanded. Justice and mercy are held to be in conflict, the one may be enforced and the other not. This supposed conflict arises when justice is first abstracted from love, with which it is in fact indivisible, and then treated as an absolute principle. But the limits of the idea of justice point to the larger context of love of which it is an indispensable aspect. When one thinks through any serious problem of justice, i.e., how to give persons their due, he is confronted by deep dimensions of integral responsibility. In the Bible the righteousness of God and his mercy are an indivisible whole. The components are distinguishable but not separable in him. His righteousness is a justice of mercy which offers salvation and reconciliation. There is much truth in Paul Lehmann's interpretation that justice is a pragmatic transition between forgiveness and reconciliation.[13]

Love is greater than justice in the human situation not in that the latter may be ignored or repudiated, but in that justice is always more provisional in its expressions through law and other institutions. Justice in human societies is both a magnificent ideal and a vocation. Where justice is truly sought, it carries an intention which points not only to mercy as commonly understood but to profound levels of interpersonal and intergroup responsibility. Love keeps justice from becoming rigid and fixed in policies, laws, and institutions, and protests against them in the name of a higher righteousness when their provisional forms and relative character are forgotten or ignored. Fletcher is right in protesting any tendency to make love and justice independent principles. True justice is love distributed.[14]

The central symbol of the love of God in Jesus is the cross. The cross does not affirm an additional principle of love to what has already been said. It expresses the fact that self-sacrificing and forgiving compassion are the ultimate fulfillment of person-in-community and the ultimate revelation of the character of God.

G. THE CHURCH, THE KINGDOM, THE WORLD

Jesus Christ evokes faith in God's love so that men become responsive to his forgiving grace and long for the perfection which is his nature. Love and faith provide the experiences which encourage men to seek more of each and which help men to perceive at least dimly the reality of God. The fellowship of those who respond to God through Jesus Christ constitutes the church. "Wherever the saving grace of God in Christ is manifest, there is the Church."[15] The church is a community whose center is Jesus Christ and whose life is constantly renewed by the immanence and companionship of God expressed in the Holy Spirit. In the earliest days Christians recognized that the Spirit which descended on them at Pentecost was the same Spirit whom they encountered in Jesus. The Christian church has her primary continuity in the historic fellowship of Christians through the Holy Spirit. This fellowship points in worship to God who is Father, Son, and Holy Spirit and to the world which God loves and which the church therefore serves and seeks to transform.

The work of Jesus and the requirements of the Kingdom of God define the tasks and purpose of the church, though the church is not simply the Kingdom. The church is both a community and an institution. These two dimensions of her nature often conflict; they should always be in tension. In the New Testament there is no radical separation of a "visible" and an "invisible" church. It is in fact a historical community of Word and sacraments through which the transcendent God immanently is available. At the same time it is a social institution subject to all the human problems of organized social life. As a social institution the Christian church is subject to imperfection, change, and flux. It is a product of volitional social activity and as such guarantees no correspondence between noble ideals and institutional performance. Consequently there is a tension between the ideal religious life and discipline of the Christian church and the behavior of her members.

Since the ultimate demands of faith are on the whole man, as we have repeatedly noted above, this total claim receives varying qualities of response among even those who are seriously devoted to the faith. Likewise there is a tension between the aims of the Christian church and the other institutions of society.[16] Members of the Church are covenanted with Jesus Christ to do God's work in history and to transform society by his spirit. "God wants to love people through people."[17]

In discussing the Lordship of Christ over the church and the world we have emphasized the responsibility of the church to the world. Because this mission is so compromised and even frustrated through the divisions and schisms in the church, the tasks of the ecumenical movement must be placed at the forefront of all church activity today. Yet, when the churches encounter each other in ecumenical action, they are tempted to become even more self-conscious and self-absorbed.

The relationship of the church to the world is institutionally most varied. In the circle of contemporary culture the church is neither central nor peripheral, but her status is variable along a line ranging from one extreme to another. The ministry and laity of the churches are in a dynamic encounter with the whole social order. The boundaries of the Kingdom are found not in the church as a social institution but wherever servants of God are making responsible decisions in the work-a-day world. As Richard Niebuhr has pointed out, the world is foe of the church when the world is self-absorbed in the temporal; but the church is partner of the world when it is occupied with temporal things as gifts of God.[18]

Sometimes the church is so self-consciously focused upon Jesus Christ and so exclusively christological that it loses sight of the full nature of the church and the Kingdom which it serves. It often forgets that Jesus Christ did not come to be ministered to, but to minister.

The church, therefore, has a major but not an exclusive task to transform world society into a responsible society. She has her distinctive work, but she must also be ready to co-operate with all forces of social justice, recognizing that God is at work everywhere in contemporary history. The history of God's work in the church and in the world is finally one.

Notes

PREFACE

1. William L. Lawrence, "Would You Make the Bomb Again?" *New York Times Magazine* (August 1, 1965).
2. Amsterdam Assembly, *The Church and the Disorder of Society* (New York: Harper and Brothers, 1948), p. 192.

I

1. Paul Ramsey, *Nine Modern Moralists* (Englewood Cliffs, N. J.: Prentice-Hall, Inc., 1962), p. 6.
2. Paul Lehmann, *Ethics in a Christian Context* (New York: Harper and Row, 1963), p. 23.
3. Karl Barth, *The Humanity of God* (Richmond, Va.: John Knox Press, 1960), p. 85.
4. *Ibid.*
5. Karl Barth, *Kirchliche Dogmatik*, II, 2, pp. 573-574, quoted in Lehmann, *op. cit.*, p. 275.
6. Barth, *The Humanity of God*, p. 84, italics mine.
7. *Ibid.*, pp. 86-87.
8. Lehmann, *op. cit.*, p. 153.
9. *Ibid.*, p. 154.
10. *Ibid.*, p. 25.
11. *Ibid.*, p. 131.
12. *Ibid.*, p. 345.
13. Barth, *The Humanity of God*, p. 45.
14. *Ibid.*, p. 46.
15. Lehmann, *op. cit.*, p. 350.
16. *Ibid.*, pp. 241-243.
17. *Ibid.*, pp. 138, 140, 241, 280, 282.
18. *Ibid.*, pp. 316, 274, 243.
19. *Ibid.*, p. 141.
20. *Ibid.*, p. 243.
21. Barth, *The Humanity of God*, p. 53.
22. Joseph Fletcher, "Six Propositions: The New Look in Christian Ethics," *Harvard Divinity Bulletin* (October 1959).
23. Here he agrees with Emil Brunner, *The Divine Imperative* (Philadelphia: The Westminster Press, 1947), pp. 194-195, and with Martin Buber and Edgar S. Brightman.
24. E. S. Brightman, *Nature and Values* (New York: Abingdon Press, 1945), p. 62.
25. Fletcher, *op. cit.*, p. 10.
26. *Loc. cit.*, see Ep. Joan. vii. 5, ML 35:2033.

27. Fletcher, *op. cit.*, p. 12.

28. *Ibid.*

29. *Ibid.*, p. 15.

30. *Ibid.*

31. E. S. Brightman, *Moral Laws* (New York: The Abingdon Press, 1933).

32. Talcott Parsons, *et al.* (eds.), *Theories of Society, Foundations of Modern Sociological Theory* (Glencoe, Ill.: The Free Press, 1961), 2 vols.

33. Margaret Mead (ed.), *Cultural Patterns and Technical Change* (New York: Mentor Books, 1955), p. 12.

34. Earl Warren, Address at the Jewish Theological Seminary of America, New York, November 1962.

35. Mead, *op. cit.*, p. 288.

II

1. *Discourse on Metaphysics,* Sect. XIV, see Monadology, par. 11.

2. R. A. Tsanoff, *The Moral Ideals of Our Civilization* (New York: E. P. Dutton, Inc., 1942), p. 374.

3. H. Lotze, *Microcosmus.*

4. Ernst Troeltsch, *Der Historismus und seine Probleme* (Tübingen: J. H. Mohr, 1922), p. 162. (Translated by Maurice Mandelbaum in *The Problem of Historical Knowledge* [New York: Liveright Publishing Corp., 1938], p. 156.)

5. *Ibid.*, p. 193.

6. See Walter G. Muelder, "Individual Totalities in Ernst Troeltsch's Philosophy of History" (unpublished dissertation at Boston University, 1933).

7. Josiah Royce, *The Problem of Christianity* (New York: The Macmillan Company, 1913), Vol. II, pp. 272-273.

8. W. E. Hocking, *Man and the State* (New Haven: Yale University Press, 1926), p. 373.

9. *Ibid.*, p. 339.

10. *Ibid.*, p. 222.

11. *Ibid.*, p. 235.

12. *Ibid.*, p. 237.

13. *Ibid.*, pp. 340 ff.

14. *Ibid.*, pp. 351 ff.

15. *Ibid.*, pp. 367-368.

16. E. S. Brightman, "Personalistic Metaphysics of the Self: Its Distinctive Features," being Chapter XV of Radhakrishnan, *Festschrift,* p. 4.

17. *Ibid.*, p. 7.

18. *Ibid.*, p. 8.

19. *Ibid.*, p. 15.

20. *Ibid.*, p. 16.

21. *Ibid.*, p. 17.

22. Karl Marx, "Eleven Theses Against Feuerbach," Thesis One, in *Handbook of Marxism* (New York: Random House, 1935).

23. *Nachlass,* 1902, II, 132, quoted in Sidney Hook, *From Hegel to Marx* (New York: John Day Company, 1936), p. 72.

24. Marx, *op. cit.*, Thesis Three.

25. Troeltsch, *op. cit.*

26. John Elof Boodin, *The Social Mind* (New York: The Macmillan Co., 1939).

27. George Herbert Mead, *Mind, Self and Society*, ed. by Charles W. Morris (Chicago: University of Chicago Press, 1934), p. XV.

28. *Ibid.*, p. XXV.

29. *Ibid.*, p. 132.

30. *Ibid.*, p. 134.

31. *Ibid.*, p. 214.

32. *Ibid.*, p. 216.

33. *Ibid.*, p. 217.

34. Gordon W. Allport, *Pattern and Growth in Personality* (New York: Holt, Rinehart and Winston, Inc., 1961), pp. 120-121.

35. *Ibid.*, p. x.

36. *Ibid.*, p. 573.

37. *Loc. cit.*

38. Kurt Lewin, *Field Theory in Social Science*, ed. by D. Cartwright (New York: Harper & Brothers, 1951), p. 193.

39. *Loc. cit.*

40. *Ibid.*, p. 198.

41. *Ibid.*, p. 199.

42. *Ibid.*, pp. 227-237.

43. Melville J. Herskovits, *Man and His Works* (New York: Alfred A. Knopf, 1950), p. 640.

44. *Ibid.*, p. 632.

45. *Ibid.*, p. 626.

46. *Loc. cit.*

47. David Bidney, *Theoretical Anthropology* (New York: Columbia University Press, 1954), p. 131.

48. *Ibid.*, p. 137.

49. J. V. Langmead Casserley, *Morals and Man in the Social Sciences* (London: Longmans, Green & Co., 1951), pp. 213 f.

50. Herbert J. Muller, *Science and Criticism* (New Haven: Yale University Press, 1943), p. 234.

51. *Loc. cit.*

52. Quoted in Muller, *ibid.*, pp. 237-238.

53. Theodore M. Newcomb, "Social Psychological Theory: Integrating Individual and Social Approaches," in John H. Rohrer and Muzafer Sherif (eds.), *Social Psychology at Crossroads* (New York: Harper and Brothers, 1951), pp. 31-52.

54. *Ibid.*, p. 32.

55. *Ibid.*, p. 33. See also Clyde K. Kluckhohn and Henry A. Murray (eds.), *Personality in Nature, Society, and Culture* (New York: Alfred A. Knopf, 1956).

56. *Ibid.*, p. 35.

57. *Ibid.*, p. 159.

58. R. M. MacIver, *Community* (London: The Macmillan Co., 1917), p. 22.

59. *Ibid.*, p. 107.

60. R. M. MacIver, *Society: Its Structure and Changes* (New York:

Farrar and Rinehart, Inc., 1936), pp. 9 f.

61. *Ibid.*, p. 12.

62. R. M. MacIver, *The Web of Government* (New York: The Macmillan Co., 1948), p. 4.

63. Baker Brownell, *et al., Life in Montana: As Seen in Lonepine, A Small Community* (Missoula: The University of Montana, 1945), p. 8, and *The Human Community* (New York: Harper and Brothers, 1950), p. 198.

64. Karl Mannheim, *Freedom, Power and Democratic Planning* (New York: Oxford University Press, 1950), p. 298.

65. *Loc. cit.*

III

1. Brightman, *Moral Laws*, p. 45.

2. Philip Wheelwright, *A Critical Introduction to Ethics* (New York: Doubleday, Doran and Co., 1935), pp. 7-11. See also Peter A. Bertocci and Richard M. Millard, *Personality and the Good* (New York: David McKay Co., 1963), Chs. 1, 9, 18.

3. Maurice Mandelbaum, *Phenomenology of Moral Experience* (Glencoe, Ill.: The Free Press, 1955), p. 41.

4. Brightman, *Moral Laws*, p. 13.

5. Lucius Garvin, *A Modern Introduction to Ethics* (Boston: Houghton Mifflin Co., 1953), p. 2.

6. Brightman, *Moral Laws, loc. cit.*

7. See Mandelbaum, *Phenomenology of Moral Experience*, p. 29.

8. *Ibid.*, p. 50.

9. The laws added by DeWolf are found in class syllabi.

10. Brightman, *Moral Laws*, p. 98.

11. *Ibid.*, p. 106.

12. *Ibid.*, p. 125.

13. *Ibid.*, p. 142.

14. *Ibid.*, p. 156.

15. *Ibid.*, p. 171.

16. *Ibid.*, p. 183.

17. *Ibid.*, p. 194.

18. *Ibid.*, p. 204.

19. *Ibid.*, p. 223.

20. *Ibid.*, p. 242.

21. Mandelbaum, *Phenomenology of Moral Experience*, p. 181.

22. Peter A. Bertocci, "Does the Concept of Christian Love Add Anything to Moral Philosophy?" *The Journal of Religion*, 38 (1958), p. 5.

23. *The Messenger*, April 3, 1956. Reprinted in D. B. Robertson (ed.), *Love and Justice* (Philadelphia: The Westminster Press, 1957).

IV

1. Brightman, *Moral Laws*, p. 98.

2. See Mandelbaum, *Phenomenology of Moral Experience*, pp. 238 f., 263, 268-270, *passim*.

3. *Ibid.*, p. 280.

4. *Ibid.*, p. 269.

5. Ralph Waldo Emerson, "Self-Reliance."

6. Mandelbaum, *Phenomenology of Moral Experience, loc. cit.*

7. Richard Cabot, *The Meaning of Right and Wrong* (New York: The Macmillan Co., 1934).

8. Cited in Waldo Beach and H. R. Niebuhr (eds.), *Christian Ethics* (New York: Ronald Press, 1955), pp. 327-352.

9. The term was introduced into sociology by Emile Durkheim.

10. Bertocci and Millard, *op. cit.*, pp. 420 ff.

11. Cabot, *op. cit.*, Ch. I.

12. Brightman, *Moral Laws*, p. 106.

13. Immanuel Kant, *Fundamental Principles of the Metaphysic of Ethics* (New York: D. Appleton-Century Company, Inc., 1938), p. 38.

14. See Wheelwright, *op. cit.*, pp. 178-186; Bertocci and Millard, *op. cit.*, pp. 475-479; Lehmann, *op. cit.*, pp. 172-189.

15. Brightman, *Moral Laws*, p. 113.

16. *Ibid.*, p. 118.

17. David Riesman, Nathan Glazer, and Reuel Denney, *The Lonely Crowd* (New Haven: Yale University Press, 1950). Available also in Doubleday Anchor Books edition.

18. *Ibid.*, p. 32. (Page references are to Doubleday Anchor Books edition.)

19. *Ibid.*, p. 37.

20. *Ibid.*, p. 278.

21. Autonomy does not mean self-sufficiency. It is an ingredient of freedom as described by Christian theorists like Barth, Lehmann, Bonhoeffer, and others.

22. Writers like Brightman and Tillich have painstakingly clarified these issues. See the former's *A Philosophy of Religion* and the latter's *Systematic Theology.*

23. Paul Tillich, *Systematic Theology* (Chicago: University of Chicago Press, 1951), Vol. I, p. 56.

24. L. Harold DeWolf, *Religious Revolt Against Reason* (New York: Harper and Brothers, 1949), Ch. IV.

25. Arthur Schlesinger, Jr., in C. W. Kegley and R. W. Bretall, *Reinhold Niebuhr: His Religious, Social and Political Thought* (New York: The Macmillan Co., 1956), p. 132.

26. Richard Kroner, *ibid.*, p. 182.

27. *Ibid.*, pp. 32 f.

28. Brightman, *Moral Laws*, p. 121.

29. See H. D. Lewis, *Morals and the New Theology* (New York: Harper & Brothers, n.d.), p. 24.

30. *Ibid.*, p. 28.

31. *Ibid.*, p. 38.

V

1. E. S. Brightman, *Philosophy of Religion* (New York: Prentice-Hall, 1940), p. 88.

2. Mandelbaum, *Phenomenology of Moral Experience*, p. 122.

3. Bidney, *op. cit.*, pp. 423-432.

4. Brightman, *Moral Laws*, p. 125.

5. Quoted in Brightman, *ibid.*, p. 129. From *Archiv für systematische Philosophie*, 2 (1896), 235.

6. See E. S. Brightman, *Persons and Values* (Boston: Boston University Press, 1951); Bertocci and Millard, *op. cit.*, Chs. 22-25.

7. Kegley and Bretall, *op. cit.*, p. 447.

8. Garvin, *op. cit.*, pp. 201-203.

9. W. G. Everett, *Moral Values* (New York: Henry Holt, 1918), Ch. VII.

10. Garvin, *op. cit.*, p. 344.

11. A. Dudley Ward (ed.), *Goals of Economic Life* (New York: Harper and Brothers, 1953).

12. Max Weber, *The Protestant Ethic and the Spirit of Capitalism;* Ernst Troeltsch, *The Social Teachings of the Christian Churches;* R. H. Tawney, *Religion and the Rise of Capitalism;* Kenneth Boulding, *The Organizational Revolution;* Canon V. A. Demant, *Religion and the Decline of Capitalism.*

13. Virtues in both Aristotle and Aquinas are habits of the will directed toward some end or value.

14. Brightman, *Moral Laws,* p. 142.

15. *Ibid.,* p. 143.

16. Margaret Mead, *op. cit.,* pp. 288-303.

17. See Mandelbaum, *Phenomenology of Moral Experience,* p. 197.

18. *Ibid.,* p. 83.

19. Brightman, *Moral Laws,* p. 156.

20. Reinhold Niebuhr, "Is Social Conflict Inevitable?" *Scribner's Magazine* (September 1935).

21. Lewis, *op. cit.,* p. 125.

22. E. L. Long, Jr., *Conscience and Compromise* (Philadelphia: The Westminster Press, 1954).

23. Reinhold Niebuhr, *The Self and the Dramas of History* (New York: Charles Scribner's Sons, 1955), p. 95.

24. Reinhold Niebuhr, *Faith and History* (New York: Charles Scribner's Sons, 1949), p. 179.

25. See discussion by Mandelbaum, *Phenomenology of Moral Experience,* pp. 23 f.

26. "Relating Faith to Decision," Department of the Church and Economic Life, Division of Christian Life and Work, The National Council of the Churches of Christ in the U.S.A. (December 1955).

27. Brightman, *Moral Laws,* p. 171.

28. Quoted in Beach and Niebuhr, *op. cit.,* pp. 312, 313.

29. Joseph Fletcher, *Morals and Medicine* (Princeton: Princeton University Press, 1954), p. 214.

30. Mandelbaum, *Phenomenology of Moral Experience,* p. 109.

31. *Ibid.,* p. 107.

32. *Ibid.,* p. 80. Mandelbaum here properly corrects the view of W. D. Ross.

33. Troeltsch, *Der Historismus und seine Probleme.* Paul Tillich and especially Reinhold Niebuhr stress the significance of this fact for ethics and social policy. See also John Bennett, *Christian Ethics and Social Policy.*

34. Brunner, *op. cit.,* p. 111. See the fruitful discussion in George F. Thomas, *Christian Ethics and Moral Philosophy* (New York: Charles Scribner's Sons, 1955), pp. 381-388.

35. See G. Myrdal, *An American Dilemma* (New York: Harper and Brothers, 1942), pp. 60-61, and R. M. MacIver, *The More Perfect Union* (New York: The Macmillan Co., 1948), p. 242.

36. Harold W. Garman, "The Development of a Theory of Responsible Action for Greater Boston Area Clergymen in Relation to the March on Washington of August 28, 1963" (unpublished doctoral dissertation, Boston University, 1965).

37. Brightman, *Moral Laws,* p. 183.

38. Aristotle, *Nicomachean Ethics,* X, viii, 7, 1178^b.

39. Epictetus, *Discourses.*

40. Clement of Alexandria, *Stromata,* Bk. VII, Ch. xi, quoted in Beach and Niebuhr, *op. cit.,* pp. 93-94.

41. St. Augustine, "Of the Morals of the Catholic Church."

42. The recent work by John A. Oesterle, *Ethics: An Introduction to Moral Science* (Englewood Cliffs, N. J.: Prentice-Hall, 1957), illustrates how close to Aristotle and Aquinas some current Roman Catholic thought in this field clings.

43. Brightman, *Moral Laws,* p. 114.

44. *Ibid.,* p. 194.

45. Mandelbaum, *Phenomenology of Moral Experience,* pp. 89 f.

46. *Ibid.,* p. 217.

47. Garvin, *op. cit.,* p. 124.

48. E. S. Brightman, *The Spiritual Life* (New York and Nashville: Abingdon-Cokesbury Press, 1942), p. 55.

49. Quoted in Reinhold Niebuhr, "Is Social Conflict Inevitable?"

50. See Lewis, *op. cit.,* pp. 130-131.

51. Reinhold Niebuhr, *An Interpretation of Christian Ethics* (New York: Charles Scribner's Sons, 1935), pp. 117 ff.

52. G. F. Kennan, "Foreign Policy and Christian Conscience," *The Atlantic,* 203 (May 1959).

53. H. Butterfield, *Christianity, Diplomacy and War* (Nashville: Abingdon Press, 1954), pp. 3-4.

VI

1. Nicholas Berdyaev, *Slavery and Freedom* (New York: Charles Scribner's Sons, 1944), Ch. I, p. 21.

2. Brightman, *Persons and Values,* p. 15.

3. *Loc. cit.*

4. *Ibid.,* p. 17.

5. *Ibid.,* p. 18. See Chapter I above.

6. Brightman, *Moral Laws,* p. 204.

7. Berdyaev, *op. cit.,* Ch. I, p. 23.

8. Thomas, *op. cit.,* p. 435.

9. Richard Baxter, *The Christian Directory,* quoted in Beach and Niebuhr, *op. cit.,* p. 312.

10. Paul Ramsey, *Basic Christian Ethics* (New York: Charles Scribner's Sons, 1950), p. 292.

11. Brightman, *Moral Laws,* p. 223.

12. Ramsey, *Basic Christian Ethics,* p. 358.

13. *Loc. cit.*

14. Brightman, *Moral Laws*, p. 225.

15. Kegley and Bretall, *op. cit.*, p. 442.

16. Emil Brunner, *Justice and the Social Order* (New York: Harper and Brothers, 1945), pp. 125, 130, 261.

17. Aristotle, *op. cit.*, VIII, 1155[b].

18. Brunner, *Justice and the Social Order*, p. 126.

19. *Ibid.*, p. 128.

20. The literature is very extensive. For treatments which relate it explicitly to ethics, see A. C. Knudson, *Principles of Christian Ethics;* Paul Ramsey, *Basic Christian Ethics;* George Thomas, *Christian Ethics and Moral Philosophy.*

21. Brightman, *Moral Laws*, p. 242.

22. See Stephen Neill, *The Christian Character* (London: Lutterworth Press, 1955).

23. Mandelbaum, *Phenomenology of Moral Experience*, p. 169.

24. Louis Wirth, "The Urban Way of Life," *The American Journal of Sociology* (July 1938), pp. 1-24.

25. Ephraim Rosen, "Self-Portrait of a Fascist," *The Journal of Abnormal and Social Psychology*, 44 (October 1949), pp. 528-550.

26. Samuel H. Flowerman, "Portrait of the Authoritarian Man," *New York Times Magazine* (April 23, 1950).

27. J. C. Flügel, "Father and Ruler," *The Pscho-Analytic Study of the Family* (London: Hogarth Press, 1921).

VII

1. See Chapter II above.

2. See Louis Wirth in Quincy Wright (ed.), *The World Community* (Chicago: University of Chicago Press, 1948), p. 36. See also W. G. Muelder, "Personality and Christian Ethics," in E. S. Brightman (ed.), *Personalism in Theology* (Boston: Boston University Press, 1943).

3. See A. Naftalin, *et al., An Introduction to Social Science* (Philadelphia: J. B. Lippincott Company, 1953), Pt. 3, p. 5.

4. *Ibid.*, pp. 5-24.

5. Max Weber, *The Theory of Social and Economic Organization* (New York: Oxford University Press, 1947), pp. 136-137.

6. J. H. Oldham, *The Oxford Conference* (Official Report) (Chicago: Willett, Clark & Company, 1937), p. 173.

7. *Ibid.*, p. 175.

8. *Ibid.*, p. 120.

9. *Ibid.*, pp. 114 f.

10. *Ibid.*, p. 56.

11. *Ibid.*, pp. 59, 206 ff.

12. *Ibid.*, p. 205.

13. *Ibid.*, p. 201.

14. *Ibid.*, p. 205.

15. See Wirth, *op. cit.*

16. See Lloyd Warner, Marchia Meeker, and Kenneth Eells, *Social Class in America* (Chicago: Science Research Association, 1949).

17. See Chapter II, Section 4.

18. T. H. Green, *Prolegomena to Ethics,* 5th ed. (Oxford: The Clarendon Press, 1906), par. 245.

19. L. Harold DeWolf, unpublished lecture notes in Christian Ethics.

20. Wright, *op. cit.,* pp. 59-60.

21. *Ibid.,* p. 55.

22. Reinhold Niebuhr, in Kegley and Bretall, *op. cit.,* p. 450.

23. *Loc. cit.*

24. Brightman, *Moral Laws,* p. 240.

25. Green, *op. cit.,* pars. 183, 188-191.

VIII

1. See H. H. Schrey, "Die Wiedergeburt des Naturrechts" (*Theologische Rundschau,* 1951, 19 Jg., 1, 2, 3, Tübingen); "Naturrecht und Gottesgerechtigkeit" (*Universitas,* 5 Jg., 1950); "Wie haben wir vom Worte Gottes aus über 'Naturrecht' und 'Menschenrecht' zu Urteilen?" (*Kirche in der Zeit,* 7 Jg., Marz, 1952, Bd., 5/6); Walter Schiffer, *The Legal Community of Mankind* (New York: Columbia University Press, 1954); A. P. d'Entreves, *Natural Law* (Hutchinson's University Library) (London: Hutchinson House, 1951); Hans Kelsen, *General Theory of Law and State,* tr. by Anders Wedberg (Cambridge: Harvard University Press, 1949); Joseph D. Quillian, Jr., "Theological Analysis of Natural Law," in A. L. Harding (ed.), *Religion, Morality and Law* (Dallas: Southern Methodist University Press, 1956).

2. John C. Bennett, "Christian Ethics and the National Conscience," Sixth Annual Alexander Graham Bell Lecture, Boston University, 1964.

3. Dietrich Bonhoeffer, *Ethics* (New York: The Macmillan Co., 1955), pp. 305-306.

4. Quoted by John Bennett from Reinhold Niebuhr, *The Nature and Destiny of Man* (New York: Charles Scribner's Sons, 1943), Vol. I, p. 254.

5. Erick Wolf, *Das Problem der Naturrechtslehre: Versuch einer Orientierung* (hrsg. v.d. rechts- und staatswissenschaftlichen Fakultät der Universität Freiburg/Breisgau. Verlag: C. F. Müller. Karlsruhe, 2 Auflage, 1959).

6. See the excellent treatment by C. H. McIlwain, *The Growth of Political Thought in the West* (New York: The Macmillan Co., 1932), Ch. IV.

7. See Lactantius, *Institutiones Divinae,* VI, 8; Cicero, *De Re Publica,* III, 22.

8. *Loc. cit.*

9. McIlwain, *op. cit.,* pp. 114-115.

10. A. C. Knudson, *Principles of Christian Ethics* (Nashville: Abingdon Press, 1943), p. 58.

11. Thomas Aquinas, *Summa Theologica,* I-II, Q. 27, art. vii.

12. *Ibid.,* I-II, Q. 91, art. vi.

13. *Ibid.,* I-II, Q. 94, art. ii.

14. Critics of Enlightenment rationalism often overlook the ideal of *humanitas* which was embedded in its formulations of Natural Law.

15. *The Pastoral Letter on Mexico* (December 12, 1926) of the Roman Catholic Hierarchy of the United States holds that the Declaration of

Independence and the teachings of St. Thomas are in complete accord. See *Our Bishops Speak* (Milwaukee: Bruce, 1952), pp. 73-74.

16. Quoted in E. C. Gerhart, *American Liberty and Natural Law* (Boston: Beacon Press, 1953), p. 27.

17. Leo XIII, *Libertas Humana.*

18. Leo XIII, *Quod Apostolici Muneris.*

19. Leo XIII, *Rerum Novarum.* See also John XXIII, *Mater et Magistra.*

20. It has also a sacramental foundation in Roman Catholic thought.

21. *Cod. jus. can.* c. 1031, 7.

22. Pius XI, *Casti Connubii,* par. 55.

23. Leo XIII, *Immortale Dei,* par. 2.

24. Address to the Second Vatican Council on the subject of the problems of the family originating with an international group of lay Catholics. This address was made in 1964.

25. Louis Dupre, *Cross Currents* (Winter 1964), p. 71.

26. Jacques Maritain, *The Rights of Man and Natural Law* (New York: Charles Scribner's Sons, 1943), p. 61.

27. *Ibid.,* p. 62.

28. *Ibid.,* p. 63.

29. See also his excellent essay "The Church and Human Rights" in Waldemar Gurian and M. A. Fitzsimons (eds.), *The Catholic Church in World Affairs* (Notre Dame, Ind.: University of Notre Dame Press, 1954), pp. 115-153.

30. *Ibid.,* p. 137.

31. See the Oxford Study Group, *Christian Action in Society* (Study 51 E/328, June 1951), Study Department of World Council of Churches.

32. See Reinhold Niebuhr, *Faith and History,* p. 92, for a fuller statement. See T. E. Hill, *Contemporary Ethical Theories* (New York: Macmillan, 1950), Ch. XV.

33. The confusion obtains in Oesterle, *op. cit.,* pp. 205-209, 138-139.

34. Quoted in Fletcher, *Morals and Medicine,* p. 86. See Brunner, *The Divine Imperative.*

35. *Ibid.,* p. 93. Cf. p. 159.

36. Paul Ramsey, "Love and Law," in Kegley and Bretall, *op. cit.,* p. 82.

37. *Ibid.,* p. 305 (Robert E. Fitch).

38. *Ibid.,* p. 434.

39. *Ibid.,* p. 435.

40. Ramsey, *Basic Christian Ethics,* p. 341.

41. Knudson, *op. cit.,* pp. 70-71, and John A. Hutchison, *Faith, Reason, and Existence* (New York: Oxford Press, 1956), p. 290.

42. Reinhold Niebuhr, *Faith and History,* p. 193.

43. Roscoe Pound, "Introduction" to Gerhart, *op. cit.,* p. 11.

44. John Bennett, in Kegley and Bretall, *op. cit.,* p. 56.

45. *Ibid.,* p. 432.

46. Reinhold Niebuhr, *Faith and History,* p. 194n.

47. Kegley and Bretall, *op. cit.,* p. 440.

48. Reinhold Niebuhr, *Faith and History,* p. 193.

49. See John Bennett, "Reinhold Niebuhr's Social Ethics," in Kegley and Bretall, *op. cit.,* p. 55.

50. Reinhold Niebuhr, *The Self and the Dramas of History*, p. 95.

51. *Ibid.*, p. 94.

52. Ramsey, *Basic Christian Ethics*, p. 84.

53. *Ibid.*, p. 85.

54. *Ibid.*, p. 344.

55. Ramsey, *Nine Modern Moralists*, pp. 3-8.

56. Ramsey, *Basic Christian Ethics*, p. 354.

57. Ramsey, *Nine Modern Moralists*, p. 4.

58. For his full reasons, see *Justice and the Social Order*, pp. 87-95.

59. Brunner, *Justice and the Social Order*, p. 89.

60. Sidney Cave, *The Christian Way* (New York: Philosophical Library, 1949), p. 117.

61. Fletcher, *Morals and Medicine*, pp. 223 f. See his "Six Propositions: The New Look in Ethics," cited in Ch. I above.

62. William Temple, *The Church Looks Forward* (New York: The Macmillan Co., 1944), p. 175.

63. *Ibid.*, p. 147.

64. N. H. Søe, *Christliche Ethik*. See also: "War and the Commandment of Love," in *The Ecumenical Review* (April 1954). The above is also based on lecture notes at the University of Geneva, November 1953.

65. H. H. Schrey, "Naturrecht," in *Weltkirchenlexikon, Handbuch der Öikumene* (Stuttgart: Kreuz Verlag, 1960), p. 999.

66. d'Entreves, *op. cit.*, p. 122.

67. Brightman, *Moral Laws*, p. 264.

68. *Ibid.*, p. 265.

69. *Ibid.*

70. *Ibid.*, p. 269.

71. *Ibid.*

72. E. S. Brightman, "Autonomy and Theonomy," in Bryson, Finkelstein, and MacIver, *Freedom and Authority in Our Time* (New York: Harper and Brothers, 1953), p. 475.

73. Paul Tillich, *The Protestant Era* (Chicago: University of Chicago Press, 1948), pp. 56 f.

74. Brightman, "Autonomy and Theonomy."

IX

1. Barth, *The Humanity of God*, pp. 89-96.

2. *Christ—the Hope of the World*, Report of the Advisory Commission on the Main Theme of the Second Assembly of the World Council of Churches (New York: Harper and Brothers, 1954), par. 13.

3. Daniel D. Williams, "Niebuhr and Liberalism," in Kegley and Bretall, *op. cit.*, p. 209.

4. Barth, *The Humanity of God*, pp. 58-59.

5. Yves Congar, "The Church: The People of God," in *The Church and Mankind. Dogma*, Vol. 1 (Glen Rock, N. J.: Paulist Press, 1965).

6. Lehmann, *op. cit.*, p. 54.

7. See C. T. Craig, "The Proclamation of the Kingdom," in *The Interpreter's Bible*, Vol. 7 (New York: Abingdon-Cokesbury Press, 1951), p. 145.

8. *Ibid.*, pp. 148-149.

9. Reinhold Niebuhr, Editorial, *Christianity and Society* (Spring 1938), p. 1.

10. Reinhold Niebuhr, *An Interpretation of Christian Ethics*, p. 39.

11. Reinhold Niebuhr, "The Christian Faith and the Economic Life of Liberal Society," in Ward, *op. cit.*, p. 439.

12. See also the criticism by D. D. Williams in Kegley and Bretall, *op. cit.*, p. 210.

13. Paul Lehmann, "The Foundation and Pattern of Christian Behavior," in J. A. Hutchison (ed.), *Christian Faith and Social Action* (New York: Charles Scribner's Sons, 1953).

14. See above, Ch. I.

15. C. T. Craig, *The One Church* (New York: Abingdon-Cokesbury Press, 1951), p. 33.

16. Walter G. Muelder, "Institutional Factors Affecting Unity and Disunity," *The Ecumenical Review*, 8 (January 1956), pp. 113-126.

17. H. D. Wendland, "Social Humanism and Christian Care," *ibid.*, p. 135.

18. H. Richard Niebuhr, *The Purpose of the Church and Its Ministry* (New York: Harper and Brothers, 1956), p. 26.

Bibliography

Allport, Gordon W. *Pattern and Growth in Personality.* New York: Holt, Rinehart and Winston, Inc., 1961.

Aquinas, Thomas. *Summa Theologica.*

Barth, Karl. *The Humanity of God.* Tr. by John Newton Thomas and Thomas Wieser. Richmond, Va.: John Knox Press, 1960.

Beach, Waldo, and H. R. Niebuhr (eds.). *Christian Ethics.* New York: Ronald Press, 1955.

Bennett, John C. "Christian Ethics and the National Conscience." Sixth Annual Alexander Graham Bell Lecture, Boston University, 1964.

Berdyaev, Nicholas. *Slavery and Freedom.* New York: Charles Scribner's Sons, 1944.

Bertocci, Peter A. "Does the Concept of Christian Love Add Anything to Moral Philosophy?" *The Journal of Religion,* 38 (1958).

————, and Richard M. Millard. *Personality and the Good.* New York: David McKay Co., 1963.

Bidney, David. *Theoretical Anthropology.* New York: Columbia University Press, 1954.

Bonhoeffer, Dietrich. *Act and Being.* Tr. by Bernard Noble. New York: Harper and Brothers, 1961.

————. *Ethics.* Ed. by Eberhard Bethge. New York: The Macmillan Co., 1955.

Boodin, John Elof. *The Social Mind.* New York: The Macmillan Co., 1939.

Brightman, E. S. "Autonomy and Theonomy," in L. Bryson, L. Finkelstein, and R. M. MacIver (eds.), *Freedom and Authority in Our Time.* New York: Harper and Brothers, 1953.

————. *Moral Laws.* New York: The Abingdon Press, 1933.

————. *Nature and Values.* New York: Abingdon Press, 1945.

———— (ed.). *Personalism in Theology.* Boston: Boston University Press, 1943.

————. "Personalistic Metaphysics of the Self: Its Distinctive Features," being Chapter XV of Radhakrishnan, *Festschrift.*

————. *Persons and Values.* Boston: Boston University Press, 1951.

————. *Philosophy of Religion.* New York: Prentice-Hall, 1940.

Brownell, Baker. *The Human Community.* New York: Harper and Brothers, 1950.

————, et al. *Life in Montana: As Seen in Lonepine, A Small Community.* Missoula: The University of Montana, 1945.

Brunner, Emil. *The Divine Imperative.* Tr. by Olive Wyon. Philadelphia: The Westminster Press, 1947.

————. *Justice and the Social Order.* New York: Harper and Brothers, 1945.

Butterfield, H. *Christianity, Diplomacy and War.* Nashville: Abingdon Press, 1954.

Cabot, Richard. *The Meaning of Right and Wrong.* New York: The Macmillan Co., 1934.

Casserley, J. V. Langmead. *Morals and Man in the Social Sciences.* London: Longmans, Green & Co., 1951.

Cave, Sidney. *The Christian Way.* New York: Philosophical Library, 1949.

Christ—the Hope of the World. Report of the Advisory Commission on the Main Theme of the Second Assembly of the World Council of Churches. New York: Harper and Brothers, 1954.

Congar, Yves. "The Church: The People of God," in *The Church and Mankind. Dogma.* Vol. I. Glen Rock, N. J.: The Paulist Press, 1965.

Craig, C. T. *The One Church.* New York: Abingdon-Cokesbury, 1951.

————. "The Proclamation of the Kingdom," in *The Interpreter's Bible.* Vol. 7. New York: Abingdon-Cokesbury Press, 1951.

Department of the Church and Economic Life. "Relating Faith to Decision." Division of Christian Life and Work, National Council of the Churches of Christ in the U.S.A., December 1955.

DeWolf, L. Harold. *Religious Revolt Against Reason.* New York: Harper and Brothers, 1949.

d'Entreves, A. P. *Natural Law* (Hutchinson's University Library). London: Hutchinson House, 1951.

Everett, W. G. *Moral Values.* New York: Henry Holt, 1918.

Fletcher, Joseph. *Morals and Medicine.* Princeton: Princeton University Press, 1954.

————. "Six Propositions: The New Look in Christian Ethics." *Harvard Divinity Bulletin* (October 1959).

Flowerman, Samuel H. "Portrait of the Authoritarian Man." *New York Times Magazine* (April 23, 1950).

Flügel, J. C. "Father and Ruler." *The Psycho-Analytic Study of the Family.* London: Hogarth Press, 1921.

Garman, Harold W. "The Development of a Theory of Responsible Action for Greater Boston Area Clergymen in Relation to the March on Washington of August 28, 1963." Unpublished doctoral dissertation, Boston University, 1965.

Garvin, Lucius. *A Modern Introduction to Ethics.* Boston: Houghton Mifflin Co., 1953.

Gerhart, E. C. *American Liberty and Natural Law.* Boston: Beacon Press, 1953.

Green, T. H. *Prolegomena to Ethics.* 5th ed. Oxford: The Clarendon Press, 1906.

Herskovits, Melville J. *Man and His Works.* New York: Alfred A. Knopf, 1950.

Hocking, W. E. *Man and the State.* New Haven: Yale University Press, 1926.

Hook, Sidney. *From Hegel to Marx.* New York: John Day Company, 1936.

John XXIII. *Mater et Magistra.*

————. *Pacem in Terris.*

Kant, Immanuel. *Fundamental Principles of the Metaphysic of Ethics.* New York: D. Appleton-Century Company, Inc., 1938.

Kaufman, Gordon D. *The Context of Decision.* New York: Abingdon Press, 1961.

Kegley, C. W., and R. W. Bretall (eds.). *Reinhold Niebuhr: His Religious, Social and Political Thought.* New York: The Macmillan Co., 1956.

Kennan, G. F. "Foreign Policy and Christian Conscience." *The Atlantic,* 203 (May 1959).

Kluckhohn, Clyde K., and Henry A. Murray (eds.). *Personality in Nature, Society, and Culture.* New York: Alfred A. Knopf, 1956.

Knudson, A. C. *Principles of Christian Ethics.* Nashville: Abingdon Press, 1943.

Lehmann, Paul. *Ethics in a Christian Context.* New York: Harper and Row, 1963.

————. "The Foundation and Pattern of Christian Behavior," in J. A. Hutchison (ed.), *Christian Faith and Social Action.* New York: Charles Scribner's Sons, 1953.

Leo XIII. *Libertas Humana; Quod Apostolici Muneris; Rerum Novarum; Immortale Dei,* in J. Husslein, S. J., *Social Wellsprings.* Milwaukee: Bruce Publishing Co., 1940.

Lewin, Kurt. *Field Theory in Social Science.* Ed. by D. Cartwright. New York: Harper and Brothers, 1951.

Lewis, H. D. *Morals and the New Theology.* New York: Harper & Brothers, n.d.

Long, E. L., Jr. *Conscience and Compromise.* Philadelphia: The Westminster Press, 1954.

MacIver, R. M. *Community.* London: The Macmillan Co., 1917.

————. *The More Perfect Union.* New York: The Macmillan Co., 1948.

————. *Society: Its Structure and Changes.* New York: Farrar and Rinehart, Inc., 1936.

————. *The Web of Government.* New York: The Macmillan Co., 1948.

Mandelbaum, Maurice. *Phenomenology of Moral Experience.* Glencoe, Ill.: The Free Press, 1955.

————. *The Problem of Historical Knowledge.* New York: Liveright Publishing Corp., 1938.

Mannheim, Karl. *Freedom, Power and Democratic Planning.* New York: Oxford University Press, 1950.

Maritain, Jacques. *The Rights of Man and Natural Law.* New York: Charles Scribner's Sons, 1943.

Marx, Karl. "Eleven Theses Against Feuerbach," in *Handbook of Marxism.* New York: Random House, 1935.

McIlwain, C. H. *The Growth of Political Thought in the West.* New York: The Macmillan Co., 1932.

Mead, George Herbert. *Mind, Self and Society.* Ed. by Charles W. Morris. Chicago: University of Chicago Press, 1934.

Mead, Margaret (ed.). *Cultural Patterns and Technical Change.* New York: Mentor Books, 1955.

Muelder, Walter G. "Individual Totalities in Ernst Troeltsch's Philosophy of History." Unpublished dissertation at Boston University, 1933.

188 MORAL LAW IN CHRISTIAN SOCIAL ETHICS

———. "Personality and Christian Ethics," in E. S. Brightman (ed.), *Personalism in Theology*. Boston: Boston University Press, 1943.

Muller, Herbert J. *Science and Criticism*. New Haven: Yale University Press, 1943.

Myrdal, Gunnar. *An American Dilemma*. New York: Harper and Brothers, 1942. 2 vols.

Naftalin, A. et al. *An Introduction to Social Science*. Philadelphia: J. B. Lippincott Company, 1953.

Neill, Stephen. *The Christian Character*. London: Lutterworth Press, 1955.

Niebuhr, H. Richard. *The Purpose of the Church and Its Ministry*. New York: Harper and Brothers, 1956.

Niebuhr, Reinhold. *An Interpretation of Christian Ethics*. New York: Charles Scribner's Sons, 1935.

———. "The Christian Faith and the Economic Life of Liberal Society," in A. Dudley Ward (ed.), *Goals of Economic Life*. New York: Harper and Brothers, 1953.

———. *Faith and History*. New York: Charles Scribner's Sons, 1949.

———. "Is Social Conflict Inevitable?" *Scribner's Magazine* (September 1935).

———. *The Nature and Destiny of Man*. New York: Charles Scribner's Sons, 1943. 2 vols.

———. *The Self and the Dramas of History*. New York: Charles Scribner's Sons, 1955.

Oesterle, John A. *Ethics: An Introduction to Moral Science*. Englewood Cliffs, N. J.: Prentice-Hall, 1957.

Oldham, J. H. *The Oxford Conference* (Official Report). Chicago: Willett, Clark & Company, 1937.

Our Bishops Speak. Milwaukee: Bruce, 1952.

Oxford Study Group. *Christian Action in Society*. Study Department of the World Council of Churches (Study 51 E/328, June 1951).

Parsons, Talcott, et al. (eds.). *Theories of Society, Foundations of Modern Sociological Theory*. Glencoe, Ill: The Free Press, 1961. 2 vols.

Pius XI. *Casti Connubii*, in J. Husslein, S. J., *Social Wellsprings*, Vol. II. Milwaukee: Bruce Publishing Co., 1943.

Ramsey, Paul. *Basic Christian Ethics*. New York: Charles Scribner's Sons, 1950.

———. *Nine Modern Moralists*. Englewood Cliffs, N. J.: Prentice-Hall, Inc., 1962.

Riesman, David, Nathan Glazer, and Reuel Denney. *The Lonely Crowd*. New Haven: Yale University Press, 1950.

Robertson, D. B. (ed.). *Love and Justice*. Philadelphia: The Westminster Press, 1957.

Rohrer, John H., and Muzafer Sherif (eds.). *Social Psychology at Crossroads*. New York: Harper and Brothers, 1951.

Rommen, Heinrich. "The Church and Human Rights," in Waldemar Gurian and M. A. Fitzsimons (eds.), *The Catholic Church in World Affairs*. Notre Dame, Ind.: University of Notre Dame Press, 1954.

———. *The State in Catholic Thought*. St. Louis: B. Herder Co., 1945.

Rosen, Ephraim. "Self-Portrait of a Fascist." *The Journal of Abnormal and Social Psychology*, 44 (October 1949).

Royce, Josiah. *The Problem of Christianity*. New York: The Macmillan Company, 1913. 2 vols.

Schrey, H. H. "Naturrecht," in *Weltkirchenlexikon, Handbuch der Öikumene*. Stuttgart: Kreuz Verlag, 1960.

Søe, N. H. "War and the Commandment of Love." *The Ecumenical Review* (April 1954).

Temple, William. *The Church Looks Forward*. New York: The Macmillan Co., 1944.

Thomas, George F. *Christian Ethics and Moral Philosophy*. New York: Charles Scribner's Sons, 1955.

Tillich, Paul. *The Protestant Era*. Chicago: University of Chicago Press, 1948.

————. *Systematic Theology*. Vol. I. Chicago: University of Chicago Press, 1951.

Troeltsch, Ernst. *Der Historismus und seine Probleme*. Tübingen: J. H. Mohr, 1922.

Tsanoff, R. A. *The Moral Ideals of Our Civilization*. New York: E. P. Dutton, Inc., 1942.

Ward, A. Dudley (ed.). *Goals of Economic Life*. New York: Harper and Brothers, 1953.

Warner, Lloyd, *et al*. *Social Class in America*. Chicago: Science Research Associates, 1949.

Weber, Max. *The Theory of Social and Economic Organization*. New York: Oxford University Press, 1947.

Wendland, H. D. "Social Humanism and Christian Care." *The Ecumenical Review*, 8 (January 1956).

Wheelwright, Philip. *A Critical Introduction to Ethics*. New York: Doubleday, Doran and Co., 1935.

Williams, Daniel D. "Niebuhr and Liberalism," in C. W. Kegley and R. W. Bretall, *Reinhold Niebuhr: His Religious, Social and Political Thought*.

Wirth, Louis. "The Urban Way of Life." *The American Journal of Sociology* (July 1938).

Wolf, Erick. *Das Problem der Naturrechtslehre: Versuch einer Orientierung* (hrsg. v.d. rechts- und staatswissenschaftlichen Fakultät der Universität Freiburg/Breisgau. Verlag: C. F. Müller, Karlsruhe, 2 Auflage, 1959).

Wright, Quincy (ed.). *The World Community*. Chicago: University of Chicago Press, 1948.